T0149322

Dances with Ancestors

Dances with
Ancestors

The Shaman's Guide to Engaging the Old Ones

David Kowalewski, PhD

DANCES WITH ANCESTORS
THE SHAMAN'S GUIDE TO
ENGAGING THE OLD ONES

iUniverse books may be ordered through booksellers or by contacting:

iUniverse
1663 Liberty Drive
Bloomington, IN 47403
www.iuniverse.com
1-800-Authors (1-800-288-4677)

ISBN: 978-1-5320-8895-7 (sc)
ISBN: 978-1-5320-8896-4 (e)

Library of Congress Control Number: 2019919331

Print information available on the last page.

iUniverse rev. date: 11/26/2019

ALSO BY DAVID KOWALEWSKI:

Death Walkers: Shamanic Psychopomps, Earthbound Ghosts, and Helping Spirits in the Afterlife Realm (IUniverse, 2015).

Critical Acclaim for *Death Walkers*

Dr. Kowalewski writes in a clear and compassionate way, showing how sometimes, at death, it is necessary to perform healing work on a soul to help it transcend. This is an important book.

–SANDRA INGERMAN, MA, author of *Soul Retrieval*

Drawing on first-hand accounts and cross-cultural research, David Kowalewski offers us an engaging Western perspective on the art and methods of the psychopomp. Anyone who's going to die will benefit from this highly readable book.

–BILL PLOTKIN, PhD, author of *Soulcraft*

This is the most in-depth treatment of the subject that I have ever read. Using personal experiences to illustrate specific aspects of psychopomp behavior and activity is not only interesting, but very helpful to those learning about it. . . . Good job!

–SERGE KAHILI KING, PhD, author of *Urban Shaman*

David Kowalewski has written a comprehensive book on one of the basic tasks of the shaman. . . . This is a highly readable, well-researched book, detailing a number of Dr. Kowalewski's personal experiences as a conductor of the spirits of the dead. . . . This book is highly recommended.

–DANA ROBINSON, co-author of *Shamanism and the Spirit Mate*

This important book is an informative . . . thorough, cross-cultural overview. . . . Dr. Kowalewski speaks with authority . . . as . . . an experienced psychopomp and . . . a near-death experience[r]. . . . The text is further enriched with fascinating examples . . . [and] conclude[s] strongly with a most important chapter on what these practices mean for our everyday living. . . . A very welcome addition to the literature.

–PENNY SARTORI, PhD, author of *The Wisdom of Near-Death Experiences*

A practicing shaman shares the wisdom he has gathered during his journeys in the spirit world. . . . The author often cites traditional folklore . . . which makes for entertaining stories . . . and experiences guiding spirits to the "Light," including victims of genocide . . . and the drug wars in Mexico. Finally, he relates the wisdom . . . he has gained from his interactions with spirits and suggests that psychopomps could be used as "professional grief counselors for survivors." Overall, this book will certainly be an engaging read for those fascinated by the paranormal . . . that will . . . appeal to readers interested in stories of ghosts and the afterlife.

–KIRKUS REVIEWS

Selection as Book of the Month by Shaman Portal (www. shamanportal.org)

If . . . we build a dancing floor for the gods, they . . . will come."
American medium Diana Paxson

Contents

Acknowledgements

I love that bumper sticker that goes: *If you can read this, thank a teacher*. In that spirit, I thank all my shamanic instructors–too many to list without the risk of leaving somebody out–who put me back on my destiny path and so made this book possible. Since they are all skilled shamans, I'm betting they already know who they are. I thank too all my helping spirits, but especially the ancestral ones, who made me possible. So if this book is helpful to you, it's because, to paraphrase Isaac Newton, I've been sitting like a child on the shoulders of giants.

Introduction

Thou must be true to the blood of thine
ancestors. . . . [A]ccept now this . . . and take a
step nearer thy destiny."

British novelist Robin Jarvis

Ancestors are big business. We see endless ads for making family trees, finding your roots, tracing your DNA back. But this is all about *genes,* not *spirituality.* The spiritual dimension of biological ancestry is way bigger and, for some of us, way more interesting. As American ghost hunter Karen Stevens put it, "Anyone . . . in genealogy is aware of the . . . 'coincidences' that occur while researching one's ancestry . . . [e.g.,] books falling open to an entry about a particular person." Being interested in just physical ancestry, in a word, is missing the good stuff. In this book I aim to bring you that good stuff.

Finding Your *Spiritual* Roots

But what is this spiritual dimension all about and how can we access it? This book takes a *shamanic* look at the ancestors, for the simple reason that shamans have mastered transiting through the portal–the two-way street–between physical and metaphysical worlds. As such, their tradition has been dealing with ancestry for tens of thousands of years, far longer than history or anthropology or microbiology, and so offers a rich storehouse of information about how to engage the Old Ones and how they affect our lives. For millennia it has been dealing with ancestral entities in a complex interplay of communication, negotiation, and even confrontation. Like I said, way more interesting.

This book draws on many sources to map out the shamanic take on the Old Ones, including ethnographic studies in books and journals by anthropologists, sociologists, medical researchers, botanists, and adventurers about the spiritual ways of indigenous peoples, in particular reports of shamanic and related traditions. I supplement this material with indigenous folklore and legends, conversations with fellow shamanic practitioners, my personal training with dozens of shamans, most of them indigenous ones, and my own shamanic practice, including informal off-the-record remarks by clients. Throughout, I have deliberately changed or omitted identities and details from these tales when necessary to protect anonymity.

I also bring in related findings from research by modern scholars. These include recent discoveries in anthropology, sociology, religious studies, positive-psychology, genealogy, and other fields. Shamans are still active today because they know how to adapt to their current situation by non-dogmatic respect for the truth–from wherever it comes.

I also share some personal stories as a shaman, as a descendant, and as a shaman-descendant of shaman-ancestors, in order to illustrate how the Old Ones might be engaged by a person living in the postmodern world of the C21st. For example during one of my shamanic trainings, we students were asked to journey into the spirit world to find ancestral souls, and then to ask them for help in our healing work.

When I got to the homeland of my maternal line, a strange name popped into my head that I'd never heard before, and an ancestor in spirit form appeared and offered to be my helper.

Was this name for real? I went online to see if I could verify it, and to my surprise it was for real, having originated right from the land to which I had journeyed. I had assumed that the name was a first name or nickname, but in fact it was a surname, a family one, which I should have known since ancestry deals with blood line and not with individual personhood or social custom. I did a little more digging and found out that the name means "Beautiful One"–and that she is! Since then, this spirit has helped me heal a number of clients.

I consciously strove for global coverage to show the universality of ancestral engagement, highlighting the many correspondences of practices and principles across cultures– the common core so to speak–that you will find, I am sure, amazing. At the same time, each culture has its unique ways to do the dance, which you should find intriguing and enriching.

The title *Dances with Ancestors* can be taken literally, since the Old Ones just want us to take them seriously, not solemnly. Serious is for shamans, solemn is for clerics. Do you know this dance? Many don't. For this reason, I offer hundreds of dance steps drawn from indigenous cultures around the world and especially from their spirit experts, the shamans.

I use the term "shaman" in the broad sense, as has long been the case in the academic literature on indigenous spirituality. Although the word originated in Siberia, it is "now used cross-culturally" according to American researcher Mark Muesse and other scholars, as a universal tradition. With this term, then, I'll be referring to practitioners of that tradition. But also once in a while I'll bring in material from related spiritual workers variously called mediums, folk healers, medicine people, plant-spirit herbalists, soul rescuers, exorcists, mystics, seers, sages, and psychics, who follow similar ways. I'll even bring in the knowledge of a ghost hunter or two. All these associated practitioners have had some first-hand experience with the deceased that can shed additional light on shamanic tradition.

In places I use the term "possession," not in the bureaucratic-religious sense of demonic embodiment, but merely to indicate the temporary takeover of a person's physical body by a spirit. The possessed person may be taken over voluntarily or involuntarily. When the possessing spirit is harming the person in some way and needs to be removed by a ceremonial depossession, I will use the term "exorcism," aka clearing.

I do not focus on learning about the past just so we won't repeat it, as historians might have it. Nor on preserving it just because it had useful values, as conservatives might have it. Nor on digging it up just so we can make the human story more complete, as anthropologists might have it. Instead I focus on bringing the spiritual gifts of the past into our present and future so we won't destroy ourselves—so we can be whole souls again. That is, I urge the accessing of the wisdom and power of the Old Ones which the world so desperately needs.

Why Indigenous Cultures?

Whereas modern people, and especially those of European descent, have largely abandoned their ancestry and may think they are honoring it by putting a few flowers on graves and saving old photos and the like, such practices often seem more physical than metaphysical, more dutiful than reverential, more literal than symbolic, and more perfunctory than celebratory.

Indigenous people, in contrast, have treated the veneration of ancestors as a deeply spiritual act. In fact the Neanderthals, thought for centuries to be knuckle-dragging brutes, buried their deceased with tender loving care. In Siberia's Buryatia today, people can still recite the names of their ancestors going back seven generations.

In particular, engaging the ancestors has always been a central practice for the spiritual specialists of these cultures— the shamans. Yet this kind of work has only been sporadically mentioned in the research on shamanism, and only rarely has it occupied a major place. This book aims to synthesize the many scattered and sparse reports, together with my own experiences as a shamanic practitioner, in order to offer a full-length study of that practice. Since systematic and detailed knowledge about these really old spiritual ways is rapidly disappearing around the world, I aim to make a small contribution to what Michael Harner, past Director of the Foundation for Shamanic Studies, called "salvage anthropology."

We need to start taking our forefathers and foremothers more seriously. Our world is a mess because of a spiritual vacuum, and at least one reason for this is the demise of honoring the ancestral spirits. Indeed the ancestors have traditionally been the key to many peoples' spirituality—seen as needed for holding the world together. Whereas we hear of many types of spirits, like angels and so on, ancestors may be our most important: In Polynesia, for example, as a study by *Sacred Hoop* Magazine found, "ancestors make up a fairly large part" of the traditional array of spirits, "playing a central role in the spiritualities of the islands."

So, I've brought together the ancestor-engaging practices of over 70 distinct indigenous cultures from around the world, such as the Q'ero and Zulu, and of general groupings such as the Native-American and Central Asian. In addition I've gathered information, when appropriate, from non-indigenous but still pre-modern and pagan European cultures like the ancient Roman and Norse, as well as from thoroughly modern cultures like the Japanese and Russian that are hosting so-called "neo-shamans" and "urban shamans," who today are promoting and practicing the ancient ways.

The Kinds of Ancestors

Take a look sometime at a tall family tree–hundreds of names at least. So which ancestors to dance with? They are a varied lot. As two experienced ghost hunters, Tony and Jenny Brueski, described them, "There are the beloved grandmas, there are the disturbed second-cousins . . . and there is everything in between."

Of course if we go back far enough, we can see the entire *human* lineage–the first humans who arose in Africa are the ancestors of us all. So, we humans are all connected ancestrally–we are all blood-related. As the Native-American Lakota say, *Mitakuye oyasin*–All my relations–or to translate loosely: We are all one family. Everyone who has ever lived is our ancestor. I don't know if that raw fact can stop humans from killing each other, but hope springs eternal.

Still, to engage the ancestors most intelligently today, we need to make some distinctions for the sake of clear navigation and focus:

{} Most people are familiar with *paternal* and *maternal* lines. Shamans advise engaging with both, for reasons I'll explain in later chapters.

{} Indigenous cultures have distinguished between *immediate* and *remote* types. Immediate ones are usually those who are well-known to us and easily remembered. They include individual family members who just recently passed away, namely parents, grandparents, and great-grandparents, as well as aunts and uncles, of both lines. They are often felt to be easily accessible at, or near, the homes of descendants, or at least the descendants know the locales of their remains. For these reasons they are the ones you are most likely to meet. According to Karen Stevens, "Most of the spirits you're likely to encounter will be your own deceased relatives . . . dropping by to see how you are doing."

You don't need to have met your immediate ancestors for them to be "close" to you. That is, such ancestors are still involved in your life even though you did not interact with them during their lifetimes. A telling story by an anonymous near-death experiencer (NDEr) makes this point clearly: "All my dead relatives were there [in the spirit world]. I knew everyone even though I hadn't met them before."

Think first of dancing with grandparents, who seem to show up disproportionately during ancestral engagement. Why so? A Native-American saying about spiritual genealogy goes like this: The oak tree is like the oak tree, and the acorn is like the acorn, but the two are unlike each other. That is, grandparents and grandchildren have more in common with each other than with their parents. The same notion can be found in other cultures. (Is this why we associate grandparents with gifts, but parents with discipline?) Also, we have four grandparents compared to only two parents, and they are much more likely to have died than our parents. Too, they show up much more often than do our eight great-grandparents, whom few of us have ever even met and, if we did, likely have little to remember about them, and so we so are unlikely to feel a lot of emotional resonance. In short, we have good reasons for why grandparents stand out. As American medium Jeffrey Wands put it, "Grandmas seem to be particularly caring about those they leave behind."

NDErs seem especially likely to meet a grandparent compared to other ancestors during their encounters on the other side. American researchers Jeffrey Long and Paul Perry found that a grandparent may well arrive to tell the NDErs, "It's not your time yet," and to give advice for living their lives, including what things "need to be done" to "finish the work." Sometimes both grandparents appear. And sometimes living grandparents and their living grandchildren will have NDEs *at the same time,* and even *meet up together* then in the unearthly realm.

Remote ancestors, on the other hand, left physical reality in the more distant past, well before we were born. They are sometimes revered as very ancient, cosmological gods ruling over a large geographical area. A common term is *clan ancestors,* while less common terms are "totem ancestors" and "ancestors of the nations." I sometimes refer to them as Uber- or Ur- or Super- or Haupt-ancestors, or as Keeper or Master or Archetype or Chief ancestors, of a whole clan, tribe, or culture. Mayans in Central America, for example, may ceremonialize a Clan or Spirit or Essence ancestor. In Korea, some ancestors are venerated as patrons of entire tribes. To Polynesians, such ancestors help the entire clan. Special reverence may be given to the one individual believed to be the originator of the people.

These ancestors may be remote in physical time, but hardly so in metaphysical timelessness. For example some NDErs, as Jeffrey Long discovered, see a multitude of their deceased relatives, indeed "thousands of them . . . in transcendent spirit form."

Other terms for immediate and remote Old Ones are "concrete ancestors" and "abstract ancestors." Throughout the book I'll be referring mainly to the first kind, the immediate or proximate ancestors, unless I refer specifically to "remote" or "clan" ones.

{} Since I am highlighting spiritual links, then in addition to *sanguinary*, aka biological, ancestors, I also need to mention, as a side note, links with *non-sanguinary* "ancestors." Most people have known, or know about, their blood lineages. Yet many too, during their upbringing, had only parental substitutes, namely those who acted *in loco parentis*, aka in place of the parents, such as adopting parents, stepparents, foster parents, principal caregivers in orphanages, teachers, and mentors. Yet such people may feel just as close to these non-sanguinary childhood providers as they would have to their sanguinary ones–and maybe even closer.

At the same time, though, many of these people, having lost all physical connections with their biological lineage, fear that these links may never be recovered. But for shamans, such a concern is unfounded for two reasons. First, they know that all of us are still connected with our biological ancestors *spiritually*, and that these links can be uncovered via divination ceremonies and then relayed to the living descendants. Such Old Ones do in fact watch over their descendants, whether the latter know it–or know them–or not. This idea is not just wishful thinking. Adoptees during NDEs have reported meeting their biological parents, which suggests, as D. Linn and other American researchers have put it, the "eternal nature of family bonds." Second, those who have experienced only non-sanguinary lineages in their lifetimes are, in fact, doubly fortunate, having two sets of Old Ones to link up with, the sanguinary and the non-sanguinary–both of them willing and able to help, and both accessible in the spirit realm. In this book, I'll be dealing just with sanguinary ancestors.

{} While you may think that your ancestors were *non-shamanic*, a surprising number were likely in fact *shamanic*. So, if you want more magic in your life, you might search your ancestry for those especially enchanting Old Ones. Family heirlooms for example, like drums and hobby horses, may be clues to your charming ancestry.

{} Finally, not all is love and light in the spirit world. While most ancestors are *benevolent,* others are *malevolent.* Ancient Egypt, for example, recognized both types, who brought strings of good and bad luck respectively. The less-than-nice ones have agendas that threaten your wellbeing. For this reason, indigenous cultures have devised a variety of measures to protect themselves from such bad actors, primary among them being the enlisting of shamans. Even when such malevolent ancestors are encountered, spiritual learning and empowerment can occur. Except for later chapters, the ancestors who are referenced in this book are the benevolent ones.

Themes

I aim to shed light on the following questions which need to be answered if you are to fully grasp how best to dance with the Old Ones:

{} Why and how is shamanism the best way to understand your ancestors?

{} Why and how did respect for them decline and with what effects?

{} What gifts do they have to offer?

{} What shamanic practices can we carry out to encourage contact with them in our physical world? In their metaphysical one?

{} What conditions make encounters in our lives more likely? How do the Old Ones most commonly show up?

{} Why do some behave like hooligans and what are they so upset about? How does this affect us? How do shamans prevent and counter it?

{} If we summarize cross-cultural reportage about encounters with ancestors, what do we learn about the outcomes in physical and metaphysical worlds? What are the major boons and banes in each?

{} What lessons for global crises and our lives can we glean from ancestral engagement?

Within these broad topics I address additional key questions: How is someone empowered by ancestors? Why do energy signatures matter? What do NDEs tell us about the Old Ones? Do we have ancestral memories in our bones? Why and how are triggers used? What are familiarization and defamiliarization and how do they work? Why do people go on walkabouts and sittings-out? What makes for a good ancestor-honoring ceremony? Why are names important? How is your destiny entwined with those of your Old Ones? How does co-evolution work? Can a whole lineage be cursed?

So, if you're curious about finding the answers, then let's put on some really old clothes and start dancing.

CHAPTER I

Shamans and Ancestors

If you want to know the secret of the universe, think in terms of energy, frequency, and vibration.

Serbian inventor Nikola Tesla

To connect with the ancestors, we somehow need to access the spiritual world they inhabit, where we can ask them personally and directly to nurture us in the old ways, rather than just trying to research and reason our way back. For this, shamans are the way to go, since they are expert at navigating this realm. So, as modern practitioner Frank MacEowan advised, "To dismiss . . . their experience . . . would be akin to deciding . . . to reinvent the wheel."

Of course you could try to do it on your own. But this would be like taking a trip to the other side of the world to visit a long-lost relative without prior googling or planning with a professional travel agent. Do you know how to get a passport? Do you need a visa? How much will the trip cost? Is the country prone to turmoil? Do you know the language? How friendly are the natives? Do you need vaccinations? How good are the medical facilities? What are the tourist traps? What is the crime rate and what places should be avoided?

Shamans know such things about that ancestral realm. Engagements with the Old Ones have long been organic to their tradition. As the world's most ancient spirituality, and a global one dating back at least 30,000 years, it has a rich heritage of honoring ancestors on a daily basis. It has crafted a variety of effective practices that are still with us. As such, shamans are well trained, equipped, and experienced in communicating with, and enlisting the help of, lineage members who have passed. Their understanding and methodologies, honed over the millennia, need to be taken seriously.

Shamanic Tradition

Shamans are able to access a variety of spirits, aka nonphysical, conscious, intentional, energetic beings, such as nature entities (trees, mountains, mammals, birds, and so on), the four elements, the major directions, the "little folk," power animals, spirit teachers, angels and archangels, gods and goddesses, assorted demons, and the like. But arguably, if you do a survey of shamanic activities in indigenous cultures, the spirits that shamans are most likely to engage are the ancestors. So we need to view such encounters as a central shamanic practice–and a really, really old one. That is, ancestors have always been a big part of the shaman's repertoire.

Recovering this tradition has not been easy. Centuries of persecution by clerics, officials, and scientists, who disparaged shamanism as demonic, superstitious, and hallucinatory among other things, drove practitioners underground, and with them their knowledge of interacting with the Old Ones. But in the past several decades, shamanism has been enjoying a surprising renaissance, so now we have a wealth of ethnographic and other studies from which to recover the tradition. In fact, according to a global survey of spiritual adherence, "Primal-Indigenous" followers make up a percentage of the world's population equal to those of Buddhists and China-Traditionalists, and in fact total 18 times the percentage of Sikhs and 30 times that of Jews. Shamanism and related practices, in a word, have been put down but at present are far from out.

So it is the shamans who today have the longest-lasting tradition of dealing with ancestors. Meaning what? They are usually the first to recognize the ubiquity of the Old Ones; to contact them publicly and formally; to distinguish between light and dark ones and to heal the dark ones; to realize their importance for community wellbeing; and to access their wisdom and power on command via an array of techniques. By preserving ancestral knowledge, they are even said to contribute to the survival of future generations. Celtic shamans, for example, are reported to have helped their communities preserve genealogies and sacred stories of the ancestors so the lineages could continue.

Also, shamans are masters of the imagination, which is key to connecting with the Old Ones. But modern people have privileged mind over imagination, and so find connection hard if not impossible. Even when using imagination, they usually write off the results as "imaginary" or "fanciful," feeling they are "just making things up" and failing to probe its deeper level of "imaging," namely receiving data from realms beyond the physical. Yet shamans know the difference, using "imaging" to see on through to the other side, as it were, and so can be of great help in accessing "the real deal."

Too, if you try to access your ancestors alone, you may well find your emotional baggage getting in the way of clear communication, especially with your immediate ancestors.

At the least, you may well doubt your impressions. An outside shaman, unencumbered by such luggage, will likely get a clearer view.

Importantly as well, since not all ancestors are Casper-friendly, you might bump into some who are stuck between the earthly realm and the beyond. These ancestors, having died with unresolved issues, may still be bitter, vengeful, self-loathing, hateful, and so on, and as such may wreak havoc on you and yours. For this reason, wisdom dictates that, before trying directly to connect with ancestors, you start by enlisting the services of experienced shamans, who without doubt in the course of their careers have had to deal with the Dark Side in its many manifestations and so know what measures to take.

Ancestral Centrality

Shamans, then, as acclaimed scholar Mircea Eliade noted, have been "directly involved" in "ancestral cults" for millennia. Frank MacEowan put it bluntly: "A fully effective shamanism must include engaging with our ancestors," since "without the ancestors, I [as a shaman] am nothing." The great gods of Korean shamans, for example, are the ancestor spirits. Okinawan shamans put the ancestry of their culture "as its axis," communicating with the Old Ones right after their deaths, devising effective honoring ceremonies, and helping in the disposition of mortuary tablets. Among Fijians, shamans have the closest and most direct spiritual link to ancestors, able to see and talk with them.

How so? Their key is the shamanic state of consciousness (SSC), aka altered perception enabling contact with the metaphysical realm so as to interact with its spirits. Mexican shamans, for example, enter an SSC to commune with the ancestors. Scandinavian Sami shamans, and Siberian Khanty ones, do the same.

Because ancestors are central to shamanism, then, you would be wise to enlist shamanic services if you want to make ancestors central to you. In fact given the long story of shamanism, and given that shamans can be found in every culture if we go back far enough, then everyone, including you, likely has a shaman sitting somewhere in the family tree. In native communities, anywhere from 10% to 40% of adults have been found performing some shamanic service at some time in their lives. Indeed, we all probably have a clan ancestor-shaman somewhere in our lineage. The Huichols of Mexico, for example, honor Tatewari (Our Grandfather), the spiritual patron of all living shamans. So if you want to dance with your ancestors, think first of shamans, who can help you fill out your dance card–fast.

The Shaman's Own Ancestors

In fact shamans have a dense set of personal relationships with their own ancestors. In many cultures, the role of shaman is hereditary. In some, it is automatically passed down from parent to child over several generations, by what Frank MacEowan called "ancestral transmission." This is hardly surprising since psychic power, aka psi, which shamans need for their work, seems to run in families.

Such transmission may occur along either paternal or maternal line, as in the case of some Native-American shamans, or from both, as in the case of some Nepalese ones. The shamans of California's Paviotso culture may inherit their craft from parent, aunt or uncle, or grandparent.

Some Japanese shamans, as well as Siberian Oroqen ones, also inherit their practice from parents, and even beyond from the distant past. For many Mongolian ones too the practice is hereditary, with some tracing their shamanic lineage back through nine or ten generations. Among the Darkhads in Mongolia, a shamanic ancestor in your lineage makes you a shaman.

Such ancestors may even be remote clan ones. The Ulchi shamans of Siberia, for example, trace their craft back to a first, primordial shaman.

Here's a case in point. My own shamanic practice can be linked to hereditary shamans. My Polish surname comes from the word for "blacksmith," a craftsperson whose profession in many parts of the world is hereditary and who is often "considered a powerful magician." The Bambara culture of West Africa, for example, has especially revered the smith as having psychic powers. So too have the Tibetan and ancient European ones. In Mongolian and Siberian regions, in fact, it is said that shamans and smiths come from the same nest or are "cousins." In Siberia's Kolyma district, "the smith is the elder brother of the shaman." Among the Yakut in Siberia, forging and shamanizing are both regarded as important for the people's wellbeing. In Nepal, smiths do shamanic duties, namely performing soul retrievals, healing, and countering witchcraft. In Finnish shamanism they are seen as transformers, able to turn sickness into health.

There's more. In Siberian shamanism the most powerful practitioners are the smiths because, according to researcher Heidi Abgey, they make "the sacred things, like drums and jaw harps and bells and such." Indeed in some locales the smiths must have inherited their craft before being allowed to make these sacred objects. The Tamang people of Nepal say that smiths are entrusted by the spirits with mantras and alchemical powers that allow them to transmute useless ore into useful metal. In many shamanic cultures, iron has been seen as a magical protective substance against malevolent spirits because it's made by smiths. For this reason in Egypt, Burma, North America, Britain, India and elsewhere, smiths were hired to make amulets, horseshoes, and knives to ward off negativity. So check for the magical implications of your name—its etymology may be a clue to your power. And remember to hang that horseshoe by your door—just for luck.

In other cultures, shamans don't inherit their career automatically, but are explicitly called to it by ancestors. Such may happen to Wintu, Shasta, and Inuit shamans of North America, for example, and to Aboriginal ones of Australia.

The calling may take the form of an NDE, during which experiencers encounter deceased family members in a sort of "meet and greet," who tell them, "It's not your time yet." They then return to physical reality with psychic powers like healing and precognition, to fulfill their calling until "it's finally their time." So, any given shaman may well have had a first-hand out-of-body experience in the Land of the Deceased, and so can navigate the ancestral realm with ease, having "been there, done that." Who better to communicate with ancestors, then, than someone who has died like they did and lived to tell about it? Who better than someone who has visited that ancestral realm and returned with telepathic, clairvoyant, and other skills to use in contacting them?

Ancestors have other dramatic ways to call their descendants to shamanize. A Korean may be called by way of possession by an ancestor. Siberian Tungusic, Mayan, and

Aboriginal shamans may be called by an ancestor through a classical "dismemberment" experience. The initiates, in a vision symbolizing the death of the old and the birth of the new, see the ancestor "tearing them apart" in order to dismember their old profane selves and re-member them into new sacred ones, namely shamanic practitioners.

Shamans in Siberia commonly receive the calling via maladies like seizures and faintings, from which they are healed by other shamans in ceremonies. Khanty shamans there may experience convulsions and uncontrollable bouts of singing, and Tungusic ones may contract inexplicable illnesses. So too in Africa. In Senegal, for example, a shaman-to-be may be stricken with an illness by ancestors. Celtic ancestors will help to heal an initiatory illness and also give the descendant visions about shamanizing.

But the Old Ones may use less drastic ways to call a descendant to shamanize. Mayan ancestors may call descendants in a dream. Zulu ones in Africa call by way of voices and visions. In North America, Blackfeet ones may lay out a shamanic path through some inexplicable sign in nature.

Shamans may be called specifically by an individual ancestor-shaman, an event identified by Mircea Eliade as "one of the commonest forms of the future shaman's election." Huichols, for example, as well as Nepalese, Southern Africans, and Dukhans of Mongolia, are selected by such ancestral shamans. The call may come via a dream or initiatory illness, and the shaman-to-be may even be temporarily possessed by the ancestral shaman. Mongolian ancestor-shamans may call by way of an initiatory vision. Future Guarani shamans in the Amazon, as well as Nepalese ones, are called by ancestor-shamans in dreams.

In some cases the call may be made instead by the helping spirits of an ancestral shaman, or by an ancestral shaman of the entire clan or lineage to which the new shaman belongs. Fijian shamans, for example, may be called in dreams or waking visions by a clan ancestor, who then provides the shamanic power to do healings or to take journeys into the spirit world.

Ancestral Help

After initiating a descendant, the ancestors may then assist the new shaman in many ways. As Michael Harner put it, "[M]any shamans use ancestral spirits . . . for help." And such ancestors do love to lend a hand. The new Buryat initiate, for example, first contacts the ancestral spirits and then receives their powers for shamanizing. Tamang shamans get powers from their clan ancestors. In Japan, shamans work closely with ancestor spirits. So do the Hmong shamans of Southeast Asia.

In fact, the *main* helping spirit of a shaman may well be an ancestor. New shamans in Korea, for example, start working with a particular guardian spirit who is usually a family ancestor. Hmong shamans have a group of helping spirits led by an ancestral Master Spirit–the father or grandfather–who has bequeathed to the descendants the spirits that belonged to Him in His lifetime. After summoning Him, the shaman calls in the other spirits, who bring iron brooms and build iron bridges for their work–assisted by blacksmith spirits. Think about it. By helping a shaman-descendant, the ancestors get a "twofer," aka 2 for the price of 1: They help their descendant *and* the clients of that descendant. They get, as it were, a double dose of the well-documented "helper's high."

These ancestors may teach the shaman-descendant the particular skills of their craft. In Southwest Africa, for example, the shaman-ancestors of Bushmen teach their living shaman-descendants. The Buryat shaman's knowledge comes from his contact with the spirits, but especially the spirits of his own ancestors. Native-American shamans get instructed by shaman-ancestors in dreams or shamanic journeys. Among the Osage, ancestral shamans teach living ones in dreams, during which they give them songs and information about powerful ceremonial sites. Celtic scholarship notes that ancestral retrieval, namely the recovery of ancient poems, stories, and traditions, is possible via shamanic work with the Old Ones. Mayan shamans too may be taught in dreams by ancestors. In Nepal as well, shamans are taught by their lineage predecessors. In North America, Iroquoian shaman-ancestors visit living shaman-descendants in their dreams to teach songs for invoking spirit allies, techniques for recovering ancient ceremonies, practices for raising energy, and methods for traveling between material and spiritual worlds. Ancestral parents of Zulu shamans become teachers for the sake of their progeny's clients. An ancestor will teach Fijian shamans in dreams how to heal, after which the descendants commit to work in alliance with that ancestor.

An ancestor will also help shamans in their ceremonies. In Buryatia, shamanic initiates call on their ancestral spirits to help them during their testing ceremony. So too do Nepalese shamans; according to initiate Bhola Nath Banstola, "I saw an old man . . . and a woman . . . my ancestors who had come to help me . . . [and] the two . . . began dancing." These ancestors then help the new shaman select the tools of the trade such as drums, rattles, daggers, and the like. Guarani shamans are taught in dreams by ancestor shamans how to make ceremonial objects. Sami shamans use their ancestors for help in making their ceremonial drums.

Ancestors seem especially active during a shaman's healing ceremonies. Korean shamans pay homage to their ancestors during such rites to ask for help with patients. The ancestors of Mexican shamans give diagnostic information about the sick. Uighur shamans in China also rely on ancestors for help in healing. According to Bhola Nath Banstola, "Without the ancestors' . . . help, not only would shamanic healing be difficult . . . but loss of equilibrium . . . would more likely arise." In Mongolia, the spirit helpers that possess the shaman during a ceremony may specifically be called "Grandfather" or "Grandmother." As the shaman welcomes them one by one, the spirits may then ask for a smoke, a darker venue, or some milk tea. Darkhad shamans invite the souls of shamans of past generations into their ceremonies; in turn, after death these now-ancestor shamans will be honored and invoked by new living shamans.

The list of helping services goes on. Aborigine shamans may receive their helping spirits directly from ancestor-shamans. The same has been found among Native-Americans. Among the Toba in Argentina as well, ancestor-shamans may pass on their helping spirits to their descendant-shamans. This has also been the case for the Oroqen.

Siberian Tuvan shamans invoke the ancestors to bring rain to draught-stricken lands. Mayan shamans may have to get permission from an ancestor to teach their craft. Siberian Chukchi shamans during ceremonies get advice for their communities from their ancestors, which they then relay to participants in a changed voice, the so-called "voice of the ancestors," and which they often do not remember—features indicating possession by spirits. Celtic shamans of old often had ancestral allies for teaching, healing, and harmonizing their communities. Western shamans today get help in their dreams from ancestors for working with the unsettled deceased. One uses her ancestors to help in diagnosing, protecting, and exorcizing clients.

A shaman can readily recruit an ancestor as a supporter because the two already have a spiritual connection. Ancestors are, as it were, off-the-shelf allies, ready to go to work. How so? Here's a conversation I had with one of my ancestors:

Q: What problems are you best able to help me with?
A: Family relationships.
Q: I understand what you're saying, at least for immediate ancestors like you, because you know us so well. But what about my more remote ancestors?

A: They can help in the same way. All of us ancestors in your lineage have left our energetic signature *on all you descendants, so when we see it, it's familiar to us and we empathize with your feelings.*

In a word, if we want to enlist ancestral collaborators, we don't need to go through all the introductory "getting to know you" and "can I trust you?" issues that may arise with far less familiar spirits. In Japan, for example, ancestral spirits are said to be the most important type for a shaman to use because they are the most intimate. An ancestral spirit seems more likely to understand descendants, trust them, care about their destinies, and feel responsibility for them than a non-ancestral one, especially if it's somehow been responsible for their sufferings, for example because of poverty, genetic disease, and the like during his or her former life.

The same intimacy holds true for the helping spirits inherited by a shaman-descendant from a shaman-ancestor. Such transmission across generations is easy and effective because, as researchers Richard Noll and Kun Shi noted about the Oroqen, "the spirits are . . . [already] comfortable with . . . [the] family member."

Ancestors of Clients and Students

Shamans use not only their own ancestors, but even enlist the *ancestors of their clients* for healing and other kinds of help. How so? Clients are already familiar with ancestral things. Everywhere ancestors are honored in at least a small way. Too, many clients have already had some kind of ancestral contact. For example one in ten people, according to some surveys, has seen a ghost, many of whom were family members. Also millions of people have had an NDE, especially in recent decades, during which ancestors show up. If there's a way to communicate with descendants, the ancestors will find it.

A shaman, then, can work successfully with the ancestors of a client. A practitioner can ask them how they are affecting the client now, what the client needs to do to honor them, how they can help in healing the client, and whether they will come to the client in a dream to provide guidance. Traditional Africans, for example, say that these spirits often assist shamans with clients. The ancestors of clients of a Bushmen shaman give power to that practitioner in dreams so that their descendants can be healed.

In one of my own cases, a client wanted information about a problem, so I journeyed with my spirit helpers into the ancestral world, where they brought me to the client's mother. She showed me a vision of a place I'd never seen before, then told me the needed information. After the journey the client said, "I know that place well." With respect to the information, he exclaimed, "That's exactly what she would have said–you couldn't have known that!" I replied, "Right, but your ancestor did."

Shamans elsewhere simply serve as go-betweens to allow clients to communicate with their deceased relatives. As Chumpi, a Shuar shaman of the Amazon, put it: "I help people talk with their . . . ancestors." For example, the shaman may use a special ceremonial tobacco so that clients who are wondering about their futures can access information from ancestors. Likewise in West Africa, during iboga ceremonies, a shaman will link clients with their ancestors who then guide their descendants. According to Kristine Blair, an American participant in such a ceremony, "I was introduced to my ancestors from Africa and . . . shown how to properly . . . respect . . . them so . . . they would continue to help me." In Vodou as well, a shaman may connect clients to their ancestors, asking them to give their descendants power, protection, and healing. A Japanese family may invite shamans to connect with its ancestors, who will then tell it their present conditions and desires. One modern shaman-exorcist sees the ancestors of her clients showing up to give useful information before her depossession ceremonies. This kind of visitation, she notes, is common.

In my own shamanic practice with stuck ghosts, an ancestor may suddenly come on the scene to help me guide them into the Light. For example, in one difficult case I asked the stubborn ghost if she would cross over into the Light if she saw her mother there. She said yes, and at that moment her deceased and radiant mother showed up, and after a tearful reunion they left together. One more ancestor gets a twofer, helping both the shaman and the descendant. Teamwork.

Shamans can also enlist the *ancestors of their students* for help in teaching. Since many shamans today are passing their skills on to others, including formal apprentices, they can do well to start instruction by connecting the students with ancestors. The shamans can first journey into the other reality to get a protective spirit, say a power animal, for the student. Then they can send that student and the protective spirit on a journey into that reality to a specific place and time in the past (*place and time locks*, aka itinerary) to find a compassionate ancestor willing to help. My own university students and apprentices have found this kind of shamanic initiation easy and enjoyable. After all, the ancestors are in their blood–literally. Too, most students are already curious about, as well as familiar and comfortable with, their ancestors in some way, As such the journey feels like a natural event, or as Celtic shaman Caitlin Matthews put it, a "coming-home."

In short, ancestry is central to shamanism, and shamanism is central to ancestry. On the one hand, the Old Ones are so integral to shamanism that it's hard to imagine the craft without them. Shamans, then, offer a rich model for why and how to access the ancestors, one time-tested over tens of thousands of years all over the world. On the other hand, shamans are so integral to ancestry that the Old Ones make special efforts to call, heal, teach, and otherwise support them.

So, if you want to transcend your *biological* roots and tap into your *spiritual* ones, you could do worse than getting out your *smart* phone and contacting your local shaman.

CHAPTER 2

Getting No Respect

Our ancestors . . . expected much less. . . . We
are . . . the arrogant generations who believe a
lasting happiness was promised to us at birth.
Promised? By whom?

Lebanese journalist Amin Maalouf

Despite the central role that ancestors have played in people's lives across the world and through the ages, today we find a surprising neglect. Many ancestors, it seems, "don't get no respect." Why?

New and Improved?

In the old days, they got a lot of respect. They weren't treated as faded and distant relatives, but as vibrant and up-close-and-personal confidants. As Peruvian Q'ero leader Benito Apaza noted after stopping a National Geographic project from collecting DNA samples from his people, "The Q'ero Nation knows . . . its history . . . and we don't need . . . 'genetics' to know who we are."

But something happened when monotheistic religions came along. In Judaism, people were told not to honor many gods, especially carven images–which includes effigies of ancestors–but only Yahweh, the jealous god (*Exodus* 20:3-6). According to *Deuteronomy* 18:10-11, "Let no one be found among you . . . who consults the dead." In fact in *Leviticus* 20:27 necromancers, namely those who speak with the deceased, were to be killed.

Christianity continued the attack. In ancient Europe, Roman pagans had celebrated special days for the ancestors, and the remains of the Old Ones were kept near homes in order to honor the deceased. But when the church came along, this cult of the ancestors was replaced by the cult of the saints, and the remains were removed from the home into church-run plots. Too, the church implied that contact with deceased souls was meaningless, since they had left the earthly realm to reside in a distant heaven, hell, or purgatory to await the resurrection–in other words, they were far away from our trivial concerns. Some congregations even forbade attempts to communicate with one's own ancestral spirits. By the Middle Ages, anyone who was thought to be contacting the deceased was vulnerable to persecution from the Inquisition.

So people started venerating only church-approved spirits and stopped honoring their own familial ones. They began losing control of their spiritual lives to the clerics. They less and less honored their known ancestral spirits, and more and more the unknown ones of others. The ancestors were regarded less and less as part of a familiar spiritual community. As a result the physical world and the spiritual world, instead of being on the same homestead, were split from each other. The decentralized, democratic spirituality of the family was subverted by the centralized, undemocratic religion of the church.

Maybe not so coincidentally, the church began to garner huge financial rewards from its own bureaucratic rituals, prayers, and indulgences for the deceased, not to mention the relics, books, and other commodifications of the saints. This profit-taking has evolved into what we might call today The Morbid-Industrial Complex, that is, the hospitals, nursing homes, hospices, morgues, coffin manufacturers, funeral homes, limousine services, tombstone makers, cemeteries, and more. Dying costs a lot these days.

But the spiritual costs were higher. For example, as the ancestors left the homestead, ancestral effigies started being replaced by religious statues, and ancestral apparitions started being called delusional at best and diabolical at worst. And so on.

Islamic clerics, especially Wahhabist ones today, carried on this monotheistic tradition, early on by equating cemeteries with toilets. Ancestral spirits were disprivileged in favor of those approved by the mosque. Veneration of ancestral gravesites was called idolatry, and burial sites were attacked and destroyed. Clerics today interfere with, and try to stop, ancestor-honoring ceremonies.

De-ancestralization got worse with the Enlightenment which, despite its dislike of religious mythology, brought in its own mythology of linear progress. It viewed the past as worse than the present, and the present as worse than the future—which is to say: We are better than our ancestors. This notion led naturally to the question: How could we ever benefit from them? The glorification of present and future generations over past ones, while maybe not always an arrogant disrespect, was at least a degradation. Voltaire, in fact, the celebrated Patriarch of the Enlightenment, summarily wrote off the Old Ones in a proclamation of dubious logic: "Whoever serves his country well has no need of ancestors."

In short, the Enlightenment saw itself as giving birth to a new Golden Age, an Age of Reason that would crush the Age of Mystery—which the new philosophers called "superstition"—between its teeth. So much for the ancient ones. When traditions die, respect for the deceased from those traditions dies with them.

This radical notion of eternal progress took root especially in America. Euroamericans left the *Old* World on purpose, viewing it as mired in the swamp of tradition, that is, as decrepit, corrupt, and fractious, in order to start a *New* World without those maladies. They left the ancestral lands behind except for occasional tourist visits. They laid out no welcome mats for their ancestors. Whatever the ancestral world did, they could do better. Later immigrants to America from outside of Europe bought into this national mythology—in many cases even more whole-heartedly than did the Europeans. Viewed in global-historical context, this was truly American Exceptionalism.

African-Americans especially saw their heritage attacked. Largely lacking a written store of remembrance, ripped from their homelands, and thrown together with members of barely related tribes, in the New World they had their families shattered and scattered to the four winds by the auction block. "The breaking apart of families," wrote ethnologist John Thornton, "as the slaves were bought, sold, and re-sold, profoundly disrupted the ability to even know one's ancestors, much less honor them." Christianization furthered the process. Clerics suppressed nocturnal dancing and other memorial ceremonies for the ancestors as "fetishisms" of "old heathen days." Repression of spiritual ceremonies by plantation owners made for more amnesia. "The American South availed itself of every opportunity to destroy the African traditional religions," according to American researcher Katrina Rasbold, as "continual oppression, born out of the fears of white slave owners, forbade or curtailed healing and religious gathering." Later in the postbellum era, ancestralism was further undermined as the diaspora from the South to the North and the West continued to break apart families, putting another nail, so to speak, in the coffin.

Today in America the effects of all these developments are observable everywhere. Denial of the deceased has led to the denial of death itself–a taboo topic except for casual mention. Mass media and their advertisers tout the "new and improved." Downright ageism ensued, with the elderly more likely to be regarded as liabilities than assets. They got less and less respect–especially after they died.

If we're looking for ways to engage the Old Ones, then, the West is hardly the place to look. But the de-ancestralization of spirituality and the obsession with novelty has already spread "From the West to the Rest" of the modern world. Today indigenous shamans are issuing dire warnings about this blind quest for the new. According to an ancestor-shaman of the Amazonian Shipibo shaman Guillermo Arevalo, "The upcoming generation will destroy itself . . . because they are always searching for new things and will not stop until they find death."

This means that we need to look back to pre-modern peoples, namely those indigenous ones more attuned to ancestral realities, for knowledge about engaging the Old Ones. Shamanic cultures, in short, are a much better bet.

Linguistic Weeding

We can start re-ancestralzing our spiritual repertoire by cleaning up our own language. In our self-talk we see the effects of modern disrespect. So in order to engage the Old Ones with clarity and esteem, we need to clean up the way we refer to them.

{} They are not *the departed*. They haven't left us, they've just left their bodies. Their souls are still around. Traditional African cultures, for example, have usually seen the ancestors as very much active in our physical world, as if they had never died and left us at all.

{} They are not *the dead*. They are still very much alive, in fact more alive than we are because they have left their clunky physical bodies behind and want to dance with us. If we call them "dead," then we're likely to forget and ignore them, or even to doubt their existence. But if we do that, according to traditional Africans, then diseases and other misfortunes will occur, due to the disharmony between our world and that of the ancestors. For indigenous cultures, in fact, death is not a state, it's just an event between adventures, between lives—and in fact that's why we speak of an after*life*. Death is just the transition point where our soul begins the next leg of its evolutionary trip. The ancestors aren't gone, they simply went through a doorway between worlds. So descriptors like "passed" and "transitioned" and "deceased" are far more accurate.

{} They are not *memories*. To people who say, "I'm honoring their memory," the Old Ones are not real entities, just imaginary downloads. But the ancestors don't want to be honored as dusty recollections, but instead as vibrant spirits still active in our lives. They are not memories, they are living souls. They don't want to be just recalled, but to be engaged in sacred interaction.

{} Except for some malevolent ancestors stuck on the earthly plane, they are not *ogres*. Yet according to the horror stories in the popular media about ghosts, they are supposed to be feared, which leaves us with the impression that they are to be avoided at all costs. But this is a very modern, especially Euroamerican, belief. The ancient Celts, for example, made sacred pilgrimages to ancient grave mounds, then stayed for days fasting, incubating dreams, and praying for full-bodied apparitions of ancestors to bless their lives with prophecy and other powers. Whereas modern people run screaming when they see a ghost, the Celts in fact welcomed them and were disappointed when they didn't show up! We also find a Norse tradition of "sitting-out" at the gravesites of specific ancestors, in order to go into an SSC to receive their wisdom and help. Too, the Q'ero people say that objects can soak up powerful energy at an ancestor's grave, and so be turned into sacred artifacts. In such cultures, scary be damned.

{} They are not *idols*. Somehow the phrase "ancestor worship" got traction in the social sciences, but an ancestor is not to be bowed down to as some kind of Supreme Being–far from it. True, some really great Old Ones may be called "gods." Yet to romanticize or sentimentalize them indiscriminately is just dishonest. They are not necessarily to be emulated. They had their warts and still may have them. In fact we can learn from such blemishes, since for sure we not only inherited some of them but are likely even unaware of it. A lot of self-knowledge is lying under those warts. Too, ignoring them disables any possibility of removing them. So, a clear-eyed view promotes connection without attachment. To confuse our destinies with theirs is a bad idea. Although these destinies are intertwined, you have yours and they have theirs. Just respectful honoring, revering, venerating is more than enough.

We're Back!

I love the springtime. Miss Dandelion with her golden locks pops up out of the snow and the weapons of plant destruction to exclaim, "Hi, I'm back!" In spite of the forces trying to keep the ancestors in their graves, they keep popping up all over the place. In fact, they even seem to be coming back strong.

In North America, everywhere they're still honored in funeral ceremonies; visits to cemeteries; passing down of family heirlooms; naming of children; preservation of old photos; payment of hefty sums to mediums to get ancestral messages; great efforts to find missing relatives and, in the case of adoption, to locate biological parents; making of genealogical charts; and DNA testing for self and family. Americans are also asserting more control over their ancestors' remains, according to journalist Elizabeth Fournier, opting for "green burials" as "a growing number of people have become dissatisfied with . . . expensive funerary options . . . ornate burial and toxic cremation."

We're witnessing similar happenings elsewhere. An online summit of spiritual practitioners focusing on ancestral healing garnered some 47,000 registrations worldwide. The tradition of ancestral honoring can still be found even in Islamic Central Asia. Muslim clerics will sometimes read prayers to the ancestors in their mosques, although such practice is frowned upon. A movement called Ata Joly (Road of the Ancestors) that makes pilgrimages to sacred sites to communicate with ancestral spirits has been spreading across the region and into Russia. The organizers act as mediums linking the pilgrims to their Old Ones.

So, will the circle be unbroken? Yes. Stress fractures may have appeared but the shape remains. The ancestors refuse to go away; they have staying power.

But people who keep ignoring the Old Ones will miss out on all their gifts. This is not good. Check out the next chapter to see why.

CHAPTER 3

Why Ancestors Matter

Among the Uighurs, the idea that the wellbeing of the living is intimately connected to the wellbeing of the dead . . . is widespread.

Danish ethnologist Ildiko Beller-Hann

What if I told you that students who think about their ancestors just before an intelligence test score higher than those who don't. It's true. Several studies have documented this *ancestor effect*. So, if anybody asks you why you care so much about your ancestors, just tell them, "My kid is going to Oxford."

Seek and You Shall Find?

So it seems we may lose a lot by ignoring the Old Ones but can benefit a lot by connecting with them. This notion is widespread among indigenous cultures and goes way back. In Vodou, for example, the ancestors are said to help their descendants. In Japanese shamanism, they give us blessings. Mediums report that ancestors accompany, encourage, and assist their living relations from the other side.

Really? It sure looks that way. According to Aborigines, ancestors are always present. A number of traditions use the metaphor of the cosmic World Tree to describe the regular travel of ancestors between the physical and metaphysical worlds. In many cultures, according to American ethnologists Kenaz Filan and Raven Kaldera, ancestors are "woven into everyday life" and "intervene in daily affairs." "The ancestors," say some Native-Americans like Johnny Moses, "are always there in the forests and the mountains waiting for us to visit them." Mohawks, for example, report that the ancestors "stay close to the earth, to watch over the living." According to Australian shaman Robert Moss, "The Keepers of ancestral wisdom of all our traditions are waiting, just behind the veil, to share gifts of healing with those of us who are able to receive."

At the same time, they are usually respectful of our space and only intervene when asked. In Celtic tradition, although they are not far from us, they want to be personally called before showing up. They "only require the kernel of the need," according to Caitlin Matthews, to be receptive to our summons. Likewise in Polynesia, ancestors are said to help when called; to the islanders, an ancestor's love for family does not die with death. Western practitioners might add that this summons is best done only for an urgent need and with strong intent, clear vision, powerful energy, and fervent emotion.

But how specifically can they help? The literature reports the following gifts.

Destiny Guidance

A major way is to escort us on our destiny path. Think about it: We came from the metaphysical realm and are going back to it, and that's exactly where the ancestors are residing, having already made the round-trip.

In fact our destiny's connection with the Old Ones, according to some accounts, started even before conception when we selected our parents, and by implication our grandparents and so on up the line. We contracted prenatally with the gods to fulfill a life purpose, then chose our parents for the sake of doing just that. Some of those parents even met us spiritually well before birth. Some mothers, for example, have had "announcing dreams" from their children before conception. In short, growing evidence suggests that we really did "choose this life," parents and all.

So, who better to guide us on our path than the ancestors? As American root doctor Orion Foxwood put it,: "Our ancestral spirits . . . are interwoven into . . . our destiny." Another American practitioner, Rachel Stavis, noted that ancestors guide their descendants. American Granny Magicians like Katrina Rasbold too say that their ancestors guide them.

Still another practitioner, Jeffrey Wands, points to the concern that ancestors feel when we go astray. They are "constantly doing whatever they think is necessary to connect us with our life's purpose" when we go off course, and are "persistent . . . about putting us back on track." For example, a grandparental ancestor will help living grandchildren get back on their destiny paths when they lose their way. Vietnamese-American elders say the same thing. In short: *destiny entanglement.*

How so? Ancestors are knowledgeable about the realm of our current life, as well as that of our prenatal past and our postmortem future. They can help us understand ourselves—not only our experiences here in earth school, but also our spiritual origin and destination. In sum, they can act as awesome destiny guides.

Here's a little example, I took a shamanic journey to an ancestral spirit for some destiny advice. The conversation went like this:

Me; The planet is headed over a cliff–it's dark.
Ancestor spirit: You need to lighten up.
M: How?
AS: Look for the incongruity in everything.

I did, and you know what? The world is way-y crazier than you ever imagined!

Our destinies, then, are wrapped up with those of our ancestors in biological and other ways. Ancestors and descendants, in short, have a collective destiny. So, with the guidance of our ancestors we can better understand our purpose and meaning on earth, especially when we go off path. Since our ancestors, while walking their own paths, also at times went astray, they know well the pitfalls, the crossroads, the dead ends and the like, and so are able to offer clear-eyed guidance. Africans, in fact, say that the ancestors are especially eager to guide us in our quest.

Too, without our recognition of ancestral guidance, we have a "hole in the soul" that yearns to be filled–a condition adoptees know well–making for a dispirited spirituality. This is not hyperbole. As African-American playwright NSangou Njikam noted about losing ancestral intimacy, "You walk around with an emptiness inside." And since nature abhors a vacuum, that hole is an opportunity for the Dark Side to fill with addictions and other maladies.

In contrast, as the Zulu tradition has it, intimacy with the Old Ones prevents us from getting "spiritually lost," and so enables us to fulfill our life purpose of "bearing fruit for the world." Ancestors, in short, are a familiar and helpful resource for sticking to our destiny. They know how we can find and stay on our path.

For good reason, then, indigenous cultures specifically call on them for guidance. To the Celts, for example, ancestors provided that help. The Xhosa people of South Africa honor the ancestral world in order to strengthen their intuition, which causes a "profound remembering" of our "true calling and what our job is in this world"—our "service to the planet." The West African Dagara people hold ceremonies honoring the Old Ones since the "purpose of human existence is to conjoin our world with the light-realm of the ancestors." In Norse tradition the ancestors not only do general guard duty over the luck we inherited from them, but they serve in particular as guides for everyday concerns. The Q'ero people honor special sites on the landscape by making offerings there to reconnect with ancestor spirits who, they say, shape their destinies. A Mexican shaman will communicate with an ancestor of clients to get guidance for their paths. Fijians too say that ancestors are useful life guides.

Unsurprisingly, ancestors often guide us through shamans. Buryat shaman Bayir Rinchinov put it this way: "Why do we . . . shamanize? . . . We appeal to our ancestors . . . work with people's fates." He went so far as to say that "if you are fated to die tomorrow, he [an ancestor] will tell you." In Guatemala, Quiche shamans too invoke the ancestors for guidance; participants in fire ceremonies are invited to call on their ancestors one-by-one to ask for destiny help.

Modern people are starting to notice this guidance. NDErs often report that ancestors meet them with the statement, "It's not your time," which indicates that the Old Ones are closely watching over their descendants' "allotted time" on earth.

The ancestors, that is, are guiding us in important decisions, as NDE research has discovered, so we will learn the lessons we need to learn and so fulfill our destinies. Psychics report this watchfulness as well. Often these guides are grandparents. For good reason, then, American author Gabby Rivera advises us: "Forge your path. Crack your ancestors wide open. By any means necessary, unearth your roots."

I put it this way: Keeping our ancestors in mind keeps us on the ball.

Healing

Ancestors have a special interest in the health of their descendants. How do we know? An ancestor may point you to exactly the right surgeon in a dream, make exactly the right medicine fall off the pharmacy shelf in front of you, and so on. Hospital patients with mysterious maladies may get a diagnosis from an ancestor that later proves correct. Native-American ancestors are said to bring health to descendants. In the American Ozark and Appalachian mountains, people may reverse a curse by sleeping on a freshly dug grave of an ancestor, who will pull in the curse from the descendant, removing it forever.

But just as often, it seems, people are diagnosed and healed by the ancestors of shamans—doing the job for their shaman-descendants. Quiche practitioners, for instance, invoke their ancestors for healing clients, usually at the beginning of a ceremony. Gypsy shamans journey to the spirit world to awaken their sleeping ancestors in order to merge with them, and then together they bring healing to sick and cursed clients. A real team effort. Buryat shamans invite their ancestral spirits to help diagnose and heal clients. Among the Ulchi, a shaman's ancestral spirits help out during healing ceremonies. Tanzanian Sukuma shamans, and Nigerian Yoruba ones, make use of their ancestors for the diagnosis, meaning, and healing of diseases. Vodou ones sing songs to their ancestors for help during healing ceremonies. Mongolian ones may merge with ancestral grandfather souls to enlist their help while healing. Korean ones summon ancestors to their ceremonies by singing songs to them, then allow themselves to be voluntarily possessed by them for the sake of healing clients.

In one of my own cases, a male client with severe anxiety was helped by one of my ancestral spirits. During the ceremony I saw my female ancestor hover over the client and then sink into his body. After the ceremony the client, who claimed his anxiety was gone, said he had felt a comforting female energy fill up his body.

Shaman-ancestors in particular may give their shaman-descendants healing advice. Amazonian shamans, for example, get power from such ancestors for healing. Siberian ones too invoke ancestral shamans for help in their healing ceremonies.

The ancestral spirits of a shaman may even help another shaman outside of their lineages. In Vodou, for example, a shaman may "inherit" the ancestral spirits of another shaman, who then give healing advice to their new "heir" in dreams.

Wisdom

Knowledge is cheap these days—just google the question—but wisdom, aka knowledge derived and distilled and synthesized from experience, is dear. The Old Ones have such wisdom, and are willing to share it if we but ask. Many writers, for example, get creative help from ancestors in dreams. Bwiti practitioners in West Africa, during psychedelic iboga ceremonies, commonly get advice from ancestor spirits. To Caitlin Matthews, "Ancestry is [a] . . . key . . . to native wisdom." A modern West African shaman, Malidoma Some, agrees, asserting that we have so messed up the world that more than ever we need the teachings of the ancestors. Who better to consult than those who have "been here, done this"? Only a fool would write off that experience–and it's almost cost-free. Afterwards, we can preserve it by bequeathing it to our progeny.

A major piece of ancestral wisdom is that, in order to connect with an Old One, we need to take the time to cultivate a personal relationship. The ancestors, especially remote ones, can teach us how to talk directly with ancestors just as they did during their earthly lives. By heeding that instruction, we can close any intimacy gap.

A connection with ancestors, especially remote ones, is useful for getting a wide-angled, philosophical view of life. Whereas our immediate ancestors are notably skilled at helping us with the "little pictures," namely the particular, the ideographic, the trees–say, a problem with a boss–our remote ones are best for seeing the "Big Picture," namely the general, the nomothetic, the forest–say, the meaning of our job. As modern people scurry around making mountains out of molehills, thereby contributing to a global anxiety epidemic, ancestral spirits have a broader perspective that can calm the disquieted soul. When it comes to a trivial problem, for example, they'll just tell us, "This too will pass." They appreciate how rapidly and often things change. Fijians for instance, according to American anthropologist Richard Katz, say that from the ancestral viewpoint whatever looks unfortunate may turn out to be fortunate after all: "What may seem to be a horrible outcome . . . is seen in another light by the [ancestors]." The ancestors, it might be said, keep their heads when everyone around them is losing theirs.

In a time of environmental crises, the Old Ones can be especially helpful for instilling respect and love for nature, especially wild nature. Remote ancestors in particular lived close to the natural world and intuitively understood its healing power. As American writer Suzy Kassem put it, "Our ancestors . . . embraced the natural cures. Their classroom was nature." So if we want to stop the extinction of species, the collapse of ecosystems, and similar anthropogenic disasters, reconnecting with the ancestors might be a really good idea.

Of course we can keep ignoring the past and so be condemned to repeat it, as they say, but why even do that when the ways of the Old Ones can help us avoid the misfortune? To the shaman this is just common sense. So, just for the sake of walking my talk, I took a shamanic journey to an ancestral spirit to get a bit of wisdom for us all.

Me: I need some wise advice.
Ancestral Spirit: About what?
M: The world's a mess—nothing makes sense to me anymore.
AS: To understand anything fully, you need to stand it on its head.

I did. The world is still a mess, but I can handle it better. If this works for you, then you can thank my ancestor (or maybe start standing on your head?!).

The ancestors are also touted for giving us wise advice on preparing for death. Arguably their most important lesson is the realization of mortality. The ancestors remind us, by necessity, of our own impending demise—an especially pertinent teaching in a death-denying culture. This is a very good thing because, according to researchers, a clear awareness of mortality raises self-esteem and sociality, among other things. Death–no longer a bummer thanks to the Old Ones?!

Understanding Our Behaviors

"The dead," as Jeffrey Wands put it, "always know more than we do." In that spirit, I once took a shamanic journey to ask my ancestors for information about myself that only they could reveal. They said, "You get upset about 'helicopter parenting' and "bureaucratic educating" because they separate kids from nature, right?" I replied, "Right, but how can you ancestors help me understand that?" They showed me how my great-grandparents and grandparents, in both paternal and maternal lines, had a non-authoritarian and even permissive approach to childrearing, which my parents inherited and then used in raising me. The ancestors showed me "YouTube videos" of my wondrous childhood, how I would leave home right after breakfast and disappear on my bike with my dog until supper, as I explored every nook and cranny along the bank of the Columbia River nearby. Then they showed me the drugged-up and stunted child of today, deprived of those joys. "Get it?" they asked. "Got it," I said.

At that point I realized how much our generational legacies influence our behavior right now, whereas before that I had been thinking, in my academic arrogance, that I had come to my ideas logically all by myself,. I discovered that, while the ancestors can help for self-esteem, they're even better for humility. My view of childrearing and educating had hardly come from my singular genius.

But the ancestors want us to physicalize their gift of good sense, to make it matter in our lives. So after that shamanic journey, I started to offer wilderness-themed university courses, take students on survival camping trips, research endangered species with them in the field, write journal articles on nature-based education, and so on. I can see my Old Ones giving me the high-five right now.

Protection

To indigenous cultures, the ancestors shield us from harm. In Africa, for example, they are said to be especially eager to protect us. Southern Africans say they are protected by ancestral guardians. Vietnamese-American elders too say that their ancestors watch over their safety. In Mongolia the ancestors of a family, right after dying, are said to stay with their descendants as protectors, but later remove themselves from the household while still being available for help when called. Hawaiian ancestors are said to guide the canoes of their descendants to safety.

Ancestral grandparents seem especially watchful. In Russian folklore the remote ancestor of a clan, the *domovik*, aka "Grandfather," protects his descendants by keeping evil spirits away. For the Buryats, according to shaman Oleg Dorzhiyev, the helping spirits "are foremost our grandmothers and grandfathers, who are our guardian angels." Modern mediums too report protective ancestral grandparents.

Ancestors are even reported rescuing descendants from the jaws of death. Many contemporary accounts say that the lives of descendants and their loved ones have been saved by ancestral intervention. But such stories go way back. A colorful tale of the Hmong says that the god of death is throwing down diseases from the sky, but the ancestors are weaving a vast cloth to catch the maladies before they reach the earth.

Speaking of ancestral life-saving, NDErs too report first-hand encounters with protective Old Ones in the spirit realm where they unexpectedly find themselves. As one anonymous experiencer put it, "My grandmother . . . said that she watches over me." Another NDEr, Margaret Evans, learned the same during her visit to the other side: "My deceased grandmother . . . protected me throughout the years."

Shamans often honor ancestors specifically for protection during their work. Buryat shamans, for example, make offerings to a remote ancestor who safeguards shaman-descendants. The African Ibo shaman says that honoring the ancestors gets them to watch over and protect us. In the Norse tradition, ancestors do likewise. Same for the Fijians, Koreans, and Nepalese. Guarani shamans use their ancestors to protect clients from White People. Quiche shamans invoke the ancestors for protection. Bhutan shamans ceremonialize the ancestors who have chosen not to leave for the Light but to stay on the earthly plane to serve as guardian spirits for their families.

Snooze Alarms

The Hawaiian and other traditions relate that the ancestors like to warn us about looming dangers to our health and safety and even against imminent death. This is unsurprising, since reports reveal that they can tell us of future events, which are later verified.

A favorite way the Old Ones do this is through our dreams, as many practitioners have noted. For example, ancestral dreams that warn a descendant not to take a scheduled airline flight are fairly common and are confirmed by subsequent crashes. One woman, for example, was reportedly cautioned by her grandmother in a dream in 2005 not to fly to London; the next day, terrorist bombings occurred in the city.

Here's an example from my own experience. One night a female ancestor, dressed in black but surrounded by a golden aura, came to me in a dream and said quite grimly, "Things are going to get rough for you." At first I was unsure whether she was a malevolent ancestor trying to curse me, or a benevolent one trying to warn me. I was especially confused about the apparently contradictory color symbology. Things really did get rough for many months, but I got wiser because I became more aware of my world and by so doing learned a lot from the struggles. I then realized that the disturbing black clothes represented the rough times ahead–a malevolent omen–but the comforting golden aura represented the protection–a benevolent compassion. To put it another way, the black clothes referred to the message content, but the golden aura to its intent. Like I said, wiser now.

Conflict-Resolution

Ancestors can help a family or wider blood-grouping restore a sense of community. We often imagine the really remote ancestors, during their lives on earth, engaged in singing, drumming, dream sharing, storytelling, healing, and praying with fellow community members. Kumbaya romanticism, right? Not so fast. To indigenous people, social solidarity has always been worth every effort, and the ancestors have served as key allies for ensuring it. For example, in Fiji the ancestors are often used to resolve community conflicts and crises. Ancestors foster in-group cohesion.

Little wonder–a community that honors the ancestors promotes its common humanity, whereas ignoring them allows for social fragmentation and maybe even, in the worst case, a war of all against all. As scholarly research has pointed out, honoring the Old Ones does in fact promote group solidarity, kinship values, and family loyalty. So much for naïve romanticism. It's called evidence.

Resilience

Want to score high on a "Getting through Life Test"? If we look at the adversities our ancestors overcame, we get more confident about facing our own. Just recall those Americans we refer to as the Greatest Generation and those nearby in time. They went through World War I, the Spanish Flu, the Great Depression, the Dust Bowl, World War II, nuclear detonations, the Korean War, and McCarthyite fascism. *Those* heroes are now *our* ancestors. No matter what we are experiencing in our lives today, they have likely already "been there, done that" and can serve as models of resilience.

In the face of looming global crises, they may also want to tell us: "Learn from our mistakes—even if we didn't."

The Everyday Sacred

Ancestors, especially the remote ones, can help us recover that old-time familiarity with the spirit world. Guarani shaman Ava Tape Miri put it this way: "Modern people think they are very wise because of technology, but they've forgotten how to talk to God. This is the biggest problem for the future, and it will get worse. . . . We must . . . return to the ways of our ancestors."

The Old Ones, in particular those who escaped the attacks of monotheism as well as the Enlightenment with its subsequent secularism, led lives replete with spiritual happenings. The sacred was woven into everyday life. These ancestors felt their spirituality on a minute-by-minute basis, not just on special holydays, and so can help us recover a continual awareness of the other side, which after all is right next door—and where we're all headed anyway.

Other Services

Many other kinds of blessings have been reported. In the Hawaiian tradition, artisans who pray to an ancestor known for special skill at their craft, like canoe building, then are given special powers to turn out great work. Mongolians report that offering drink to the ancestors enhances psychic powers. Ancestors are also said to help us find lost objects. Native-American ancestors are said to bring rain, entertainment for children, and information, including personal messages. The Old Ones are also said to comfort us in times of stress and sorrow. And I'm sure we've just scratched the surface here.

Co-Evolution

These, then, are the many ways our ancestors serve us. But do the Old Ones have needs of their own that we might fulfill? Many indigenous cultures say so, proposing that it is not only we who are spiritually evolving, but that the ancestors are too and we are a key part of that growth. The afterlife then, as Native-American Menominee shaman Gemma Benton put it, is not a static state but a dynamic process: "Ancestors grow as we grow" and "As we grow we get to bring them along." We don't travel through life in a private car, we're on a passenger train.

Some modern practitioners agree. According to American medium Theresa Caputo, "Your loved ones who've crossed over . . . know when you're speaking to them, and your prayers send them energy to help them on their journey on the other side." According to spiritual writer Susan Martinez, by letting the ancestors help us, we are helping them evolve to a higher realm, for the soul only progresses to that realm by helping those in a lower one. American medium Patrick Mathews echoes this notion; as he told one client, by "helping you . . . [the deceased's] soul too will grow." The ancestors, in short, are evolving–growing spiritually–just as we are. We are all co-progressing–*we are co-evolutionists.*

In Japanese shamanism, for example, deceased spirits evolve in the afterlife by receiving tribute from their descendants (or other sympathetic humans if the spirits had no blood descendants), and in turn will help their descendants evolve in their earthly lives. The ancient Greeks felt that the Old Ones were aided by efforts on their behalf. In African shamanism, offering positive energy to ancestors helps their afterlife evolution. Southern African shamans say that helping an ancestor in this way is their "responsibility to heal their lineage." To a Vodou practitioner, if we ask the ancestors for help, they'll do positive things for us, which enables them to evolve spiritually in the afterlife. Helping us, in short, helps themselves. Hispanics across North and South America and elsewhere, during the Day of the Dead festival, assist the ancestors along on their spiritual journeys by leaving some possessions of the deceased at their graves and other practices. Such mutual aid, it is said, strengthens the bonds between ancestors and descendants. A Chinese shaman, in a special ceremony, may bring in spirit help to alleviate the sufferings of the participants' ancestors, so as to lift these Old Ones to a higher realm in their afterlives. Ancestral possession of participants during this ceremony, according to Canadian researcher Jordan Paper, "cement[s] a spiritual relationship between living and dead members of the clan." And as Theresa Caputo noted, the more we and our ancestors co-evolve spiritually, the stronger the future communication links.

In short, we and the ancestors co-evolve into higher spiritual realms—or not. Hell is being stuck. We need each other to move along. We are soul family, watching out for each other. The ancestors are our *spiritual* family—far more than just a *biological* one. *Together we form a transgenerational team.*

CHAPTER 4

Connecting in the Physical Realm

*If you remember your ancestors, they can cross
over and be with you again.*

American musician Anthony Gonzalez

To access these gifts, shamans have come up with an array of
specific practices for encouraging contact with the donors. By
walking the razor's edge between ordinary and nonordinary
realities, they are able to access both of the realms. That is,
some practices can be used in normal physical reality to invite
the ancestors here from their world, while others can take
us into non-normal metaphysical reality to greet them there
in their world. As Jeffrey Wands put it, "The door to the
spirit world opens both ways." In this chapter and the next,
you'll find out how to encourage such close encounters of the
ancestral kind.

But shamans, like Western practitioner Christina Pratt,
know the importance of setting boundaries for engagement.
The ancestors need to be told specifically, clearly, and strongly
who is invited to the encounter, as well as when, where, how,
and why. Otherwise, overeager and maybe less than benevolent
ones may wind up in your life unexpectedly and disruptively.

This chapter shows specific practices in the physical realm for promoting contact; the subsequent chapter, in the metaphysical one. All these ways not only lower our modern amnesia about the Old Ones, but also close the gap between the natural and the supernatural, thereby enabling the linking of our physical reality with a "closely related" metaphysical one.

Shrines

A key principle for bringing the Old Ones into our reality is what I call the *familiarizing effect*, namely attracting desired ancestors to a scene by making it recognizable and comfortable. American researcher Virlana Tkacz put it this way: Ancestors feel "most comfortable in [their] traditional surroundings."

Many shamanic traditions then, like the Mayan, Siberian, and Mongolian, use some version of a small handmade "spirit house" where helping spirits can hang out, often in or near the family household. Malay tribespeople, for example, during a funeral for a family member, erect a small "soul house" for the deceased near the foot of the grave. In the Japanese tradition of shugendo, shamans build small structures for the ancestors throughout the country where they hold commemorative events.

The most common way to host the ancestors is to set up, at home, a family shrine, aka altar or (in Spanish) *mesa*, for the sake of convenient and regular honoring. Here you can place objects that will please the ancestors, such as photographs, objects they left you in their will such as rings and necklaces, hobby articles like crochet needles, and so on. These items not only reconnect us with their lives, but are said to act as *positive triggers* enticing them to come and check things out.

Ancient Romans too had familial shrines for the Old Ones, and upon leaving the home would bade the spirits farewell. Then they would set off on the right foot–setting off on the left (the *sinister* one) would bring bad luck.

In West Africa individual families have a special shrine inhabited, it is thought, by the founder of the lineage. It may be carved in the likeness of the founder and must be tended to and cared for. Vodou practitioners honor the *govi*–a receptacle said to contain the ancestor's soul–with food from the descendants, who may call upon that soul for guidance, wisdom, and warning. Hoodoo practitioners in the U.S. South build ancestral altars at which money is placed. They also put a candle there. As I've heard a number of shamans say, spirits are attracted to a flame.

The Huichols hold a ceremony to capture an ancestor in a small crystal, which is then put at their shrines so the spirit can be physically present in the family. At the shrines of Mongolian shamans are laid strips of cloth to signify their ancestors.

So, as the movie *Field of Dreams* might ask: If you build it, will they come?

Flowers

In many parts of the world the ancestors have been honored with flowers, especially at their shrines or graves. Ancient Romans, for example, placed roses at gravesites during their Rosalia festival. Today in the USA on Memorial Day, millions place flowers at the gravesites of their immediate ancestors. Why flowers? I think I know, because for two summers I worked my way through college at a large urban cemetery where, starting a week after Memorial Day, our grounds crew was tasked with clearing flowers from thousands of graves, giving me plenty of quiet time to ponder ancestral floral symbology:

{} *Fertility*. Flowers represent the reproductive high point of a plant species, telling us that without the fecundity of our ancestors, we wouldn't even be here to enjoy our lives. So they automatically tell the ancestors, "We appreciate you!" Too, they forecast the future of that plant species—its soon-to-be arriving seeds—and so tell the ancestors, "You're living on!" Also, by symbolizing the new life that will arise, they tell us that we too will have a new—after—life, and so say to the ancestors, "We'll join you soon!"

{} *Fragrance*. I do a lot of wildlife tracking and sometimes come across the rotting carcasses of dead animals, whose smell is hardly floral. But sometimes I also step on plants with wonderful scents, like mints and pineapple weed, whose sweet aroma is opposite that of death. Flowers, then, tell the ancestors that, while we know about the end of their physical existence, we realize they live on, just in a different dimension. And don't be surprised if they return the favor by sending you floral fragrances, especially right after their passing into the afterlife.

{} *Color*. Dying people are often described as having the "pallor of death," a dull grey hue without any glow or vibrancy. Flowers, on the other hand, blaze with vivid color and vitality. They express our desire that the Old Ones are looking and feeling just as marvelous.

{} *Beauty*. I have a robust stand of wild roses in my yard, and I'm always amazed at the variety of wildlife they attract. Flowers radiate a splendor totally opposite the unappealing pastiness of a corpse, inviting butterflies, hummingbirds, and even wild humans like me. They tell the ancestors, "We cherish the loveliness of your souls!"

Shamans will advise that, at such floral sites, the *spirits* of the plants themselves be invoked to bless the ancestors and descendants alike.

Spirit Plates

Periodically you can put out, at your shrine or elsewhere, a plate of your ancestor's favorite food, especially an ethnic dish like pasta for an Italian ancestor. In India, for example, the recently deceased are honored with food offerings. In Ulchi culture, according to Siberian researcher Jan van Ysslestyne, "You must always feed your spirits or they may cause physical and psychological ills." Korean shamans, for the same reason, during funeral ceremonies provide a variety of delicacies for the deceased.

Buryat shamans say that we should put out such food in order for the ancestors and their descendants "to have fun." As one of their chants goes, "Oh, great family tree . . . in heaven, descend as the master and taste my offering." Cooked food is said to be especially appealing. And don't forget the booze (unless the ancestor was addicted)—after all it is a *spirit* plate. The ancient Greeks, for example, left wine on ancestral gravesites during their regular visits. Like I said, serious but not solemn.

Trees

Early Europeans planted a tree seedling next to the structure where a family member died, or dedicated an existing tree to the member's soul by carving its initials on the trunk. Likewise Malay tribespeople, during funeral ceremonies, plant fruit trees around the new ancestor's grave, then lay out for the soul some betel leaf to chew and tobacco to smoke.

This kind of ceremony symbolizes the ancestor's new life, reminding the survivors that the ancestor lives on. In fact in many parts of the world, trees are viewed as dwelling places for spirits in general.

Mortuary Tablets

In parts of Asia, a family may craft a small flat sheet of some material with the names of the ancestors inscribed. On the property of some Asian temples are built small structures on which these tablets are hung. Some indigenes in Papua New Guinea also make mortuary boards for their ancestral shrines. If you decide to make your own, you might think of using the script of the ancestor's native language if possible and appropriate.

Effigies

In many indigenous cultures, artifacts of some kind are used to epitomize and hold an ancestral spirit. Shamans worldwide will make small statues, aka dolls or totems or fetishes, out of wood, wax, clay or other material, to signify an Old One. The objects may be representational or symbolic of the ancestor.

In West Africa, for example, the Fang people make such effigies, as do the Panamanian Kunas. In the Hawaiian tradition, a small carved image is put in a family shrine to serve as a resting place for the ancestor. Yokuts in California make effigy dolls to use in mourning ceremonies. Mayans make small or large wooden, metal, stone, or plaster effigies of very ancient ancestors. Ulchi and Udeghe shamans in Siberia make special ones to epitomize their ancestor-shamans. Khanty shamans there carve wooden ones of ancestor-shamans and place them in special forest groves where cooked food is offered. Some indigenes in Papua New Guinea decorate the skull of an ancestor for remembrance ceremonies–now there's a representational effigy for you!

Some of the best known effigies are those of the Native-American Hopi, who make so-called kachina dolls epitomizing ancestors, to whom prayer sticks are offered for the sake of bringing precipitation to parched lands. Masked participants embodying the ancestors may then honor the Old Ones in a rainmaking dance. The kachinas also carry messages from the living to the ancestors in order to harmonize the two worlds.

Effigies can stand for immediate ancestors but also more remote ones, like a single Chief Clan Ancestor. They may even epitomize all the key ancestors of one's clan, as on a large totem pole. The Ulchi construct such collective effigies, and have strict rules about making them. Quite well known too are the almost 1000 huge Moai effigies made by the indigenous people of Easter Island. Some indigenes in Papua New Guinea also make ancestral statues. If you're planning a big family or clan ceremony, you might construct a large mortuary pole like that of the Native-American Haida. Another option is to make a clan crest.

You can carry out a variety of practices with your effigy. The Ulchi, for example, sing the ancestral spirit into the effigy and then have "spirit parties" with it. They see their effigies as "the physical bodies of the spirits," washing them and giving them new clothes, and speaking with them in order to find out about the afterlife.

Shamans may take advantage of the power of effigies when healing clients. Ulchi shamans, for example, may ask a client to make an small effigy of a helpful ancestor to carry or wear for a certain time.

Shamans also make effigies of the objects the ancestors may find useful in their afterlives. The Japanese, for example, make figurines of horses for their ancestors to ride while traveling between material and immaterial realms

You might consider taking the effigies of your ancestors to their favorite "haunts." As a kid I was a huge baseball fan, and loved talking with my now-deceased father about his favorite player, Hall-of-Famer Ted Williams of the Boston Red Sox. If you've ever lived in Boston, you'll know that he was also no fan of the New York Yankees. So, to connect with my dad, I might make a small effigy, fly to Boston, go to Fenway Park for a Yankee game, and root my heart out for the Red Sox. Whenever a Bosox batter gets a hit, or a pitcher gets a strikeout, I might take out the effigy and give him a high-five. He would love that. Like I said, serious but not solemn.

R & D

Today's shaman might recommend an online search of the earthly lives of your ancestors:

{} *Genealogy.* You can chart your family tree for yourself and your progeny, including the use of DNA data. Recall, though, that ancestors are about more than just blood. Pay special attention to their names. For a shaman, words are important, but names are especially so. Dig into their original meanings, which may offer clues to the dynamics of your own soul. Later, when you want to connect, use *name invocation*, speaking the appellations aloud. Whereas in modern culture a name is usually just a legal or sentimental label, in indigenous ones it's a powerful entity, enabling the speaker to make present the so-named spirit. Picture a taut bungee cord with you hooked at one end, and an ancestor hooked at the other but held in place by a latch. When you speak the name, the latch releases and the ancestor springs to your side. Researchers in fact have shown that the indigenes were on to something. They found that, in a noisy crowded room, we can easily pick out our name being called over other words being spoken at an equal volume and distance away. Names have attractive power.

{} *Historical research.* You can look into the story of your ancestral land and culture. Mohawk shamans, for example, have founded a spiritual community to retrieve the old ways of their ancestors.

{} *Traumas.* Pay special attention to any dramatic and distressing events that your Old Ones experienced, as individuals or as a collective. Knowing about these traumas not only helps you understand them better, but at the epigenetic level you may well have inherited their stress responses like fear, guilt, depression, and the like. That is, when your ancestors were traumatized, in order to deal with that stress their genes changed, and then these genes were passed on to their descendants–like you. Call it "inherited PTSD of the ancestral [epi]genetic kind." These inherited responses might then be healed by shamans, so you won't be passing them on to your progeny.

{} *Language learning.* Some people connect with their ancestry by learning the language of the old country. This skill might then be used, for example, to compose a calling song to access the Old Ones, perhaps with ancient instruments as accompaniment.

Pilgrimage

Although modern pilgrimages usually take the form of rare treks to some religious holy place, in ancient times they were standard practice for honoring the ancestors. You can do the same. Since the trip incurs financial and physical costs, it shows the Old Ones that you are serious about their afterlives. It also mythically mirrors your spiritual journey from your earthly life now on this side to your afterlife then on the other side—when and where you will join them.

You might, for example, travel to the ancestral homelands you've never seen before, and especially to gravesites. Just call it an "ancestral vacation." Why do it? Modern pilgrims on such treks report recognizing the lands as familiar and already inside themselves; seeing the sites as part of why they are who they are; and hearing the places speak to their hearts. Many are also healed by releasing grief about the traumas experienced by their ancestors there.

Too, since ancestral spirits are closely linked to their native lands, you may find it easier to connect with them there. If you can't go physically, you can download photos of the lands you would like to visit and envision a fun trip there in spirit. You may also be able to download, from cemetery webpages, photos of gravesites to use on this "spirit pilgrimage." The ancestors will "get it."

At the gravesites you can leave offerings, asking to be taught and strengthened. Tobacco and alcohol always work (again unless the ancestors were addicted). Think of the tobacco spirit as a defense against negative energies, and the alcohol spirit as an Arch- or Uber-Spirit signifying all the plant spirits. Polynesians leave such gifts, while Mexicans during the Day of the Dead make offerings of flowers, tobacco, and alcohol. Fijians say that universal energy, aka *chi*, will manifest most strongly where the ancestors are buried. During the Japanese Bon festival, celebrants invite and look forward to meeting their deceased relatives again, and so clear the roads from their houses to the graves to ease the passage. Ancient Europeans went to ancestral gravesites to ask for guidance, using them as divination oracles. The Celts for example got important information from the stories, as they put it, "told by the bones" of their ancestors.

In a number of cultures the ancestors reside on mountain tops. In Japan, for example, some descendants pilgrimage there to make offerings to their Old Ones.

The Honoring Ceremony

Peoples around the world have come up with special ceremonies for episodic display of reverence, and among indigenous cultures, these events are usually led by shamans. Such has been the case, for example, among Tuvan, Buryat, Korean, and Chilean Mapuche practitioners. Chinese ones hold a special ceremony to give offerings, during which they may be possessed by the "Chief" ancestral recipient of the gifts. A modern shaman might make use of photographs of the ancestors, recordings of their favorite music, and so on during the event. A Hoodoo practitioner may use dirt from the graves of ancestors to celebrate their blessings.

Many of these ceremonies today have roots reaching deep into the past, and some have even been transmitted to descendants in mysterious ways. Some biologists speak of a "collective memory" created when many people engage in some activity, namely a "pool of experience" available to subsequent generations and manifesting in their lives. Especially when that activity is a ceremony, this "pool" operates as a "presence of the past." Indeed participants "think they're reconnecting with those who did it in the first place, as well as with those who've done it ever since over the generations–it's a connection across time. In tribal traditions, this connection is taken for granted as a key part of the whole culture. In our [modern] world . . . [which is] more ahistorical, most people think that society is just the living, but almost all traditional views of society include the ancestors as well as the descendants, and through rituals [they are] . . . linked to the whole tradition." So if you feel you have ancestral memories in your bones, you'd be foolish to dismiss them.

Shamans prefer to *ask the ancestors themselves* what kind of ceremony they want, instead of making one up. Dukhan shamans, for example, advise doing a ceremony only when the spirits say it's time. You can enlist a shaman to derive the ceremony in this way for you, since they are experienced in such work. When making your request to the Old Ones, seek out all the basic details for the event, for example exactly where, when, what kind of music, whom to invite, what kinds of food and drink, and so on.

You can hold the ceremony alone, but shamans will advise, if at all possible, to plan a group event, Many humans joining together with one mind and one heart have especially powerful effects, as shown in experiments by the Princeton Engineering Anomalies Research group. Too, the communal honoring of *common* ancestors brings blood-related descendants together, helping to smooth out frictions within family and clan and so to serve integration.

Shamans also encourage artistic creativity. You can wear historical ethnic clothes, especially when honoring your remote ancestors—a costume party ancestral-style. The Yupiit people of Alaska, for example, during their "Feasts of the Dead" for the living namesake of a deceased relative, make use of elaborate clothing and food. Ancient Romans conducted a sort of "reburial" ceremony, during which they offered food and flowers for the deceased. And don't forget those symbols, A Norse tradition uses runes to connect with the ancestors. Huichols, for their part, offer traditional yarn paintings.

Shamans prefer to ceremonialize at special spots in nature, especially wild nature, and on special occasions. That is, they seek out *power places* and *power times*. The ancient Khmers of Cambodia, as well as the Mayans, Yoruba, and Dagara, have used the energies of power places—sites with a high level of *chi* energy such as waterfalls and caves—to access ancestral spirits. Ulchi shamans make use of such sites to communicate with their clan's ancestors in ceremony, during which they may sing to participants the conversations they are having with these spirits.

Power times include transition points between the seasons, namely solstices and equinoxes, and symbolic days, like Father and Mother's days, anniversaries of wedding and graduation, and especially birthdays. In ancient Rome, for example, deceased family members were honored on the day of their birth.

If you missed the last rite for an ancestor, you can ask a shaman to hold one for you or you can hold one yourself. You can, for instance, construct a make-shift "coffin," use a homemade effigy as a "body," and so on. The ancestor can be asked what s/he would like to be done during the ceremony, for example what *elemental nature-spirit* to use for disposing of the "remains," say Earth for a burial or Fire for a cremation. I've found such "make-up last rites" to be very moving, especially for letting go of any resentment against the ancestor.

Music

Music such as song and chant has always played a key role in shamanism across the world. But it is far more than just an abstract collection of sounds, it is a purposeful event, a road that takes you somewhere you want to go. "A song," say the Yaminahua shamans of Peru, "is a path—you make it straight and clean, then you walk along it."

Music is an especially important road for meeting up with the ancestors. Not only is song, for example, "a bridge to the other realm," as Western researchers Constance Graud and Annette Host put it, but more specifically it "has the ability to open doors . . . so we can talk with our ancestors." Since it bypasses the logical mind, in the words of Caitlin Matthews, it can "contact the deep ancestral memory directly." *But get funeral dirges out of your mind.* If you were an ancestor, would you want to be greeted by your living descendants with depressing music? Please!

Ulchi shamans use song to communicate with ancestors. At ayahuasca ceremonies in the Amazon special songs, called *icaros,* are sung in order to summon ancestral spirits for the participants. Ancient Celtic Druids sang or chanted ancestral lore for their communities. Some Ika and Kogi people of Colombia will stay up all night in ceremony chewing coca leaves and chanting the names of the Old Ones. Some participants bend towards the earth while blowing on coca leaves in order to feed the essence of the plant to the buried ancestral souls. (Will deceased marijuana fans be hoping a descendant will be thoughtful enough to bend towards the earth while blowing on *Cannibis* leaves to feed their souls?)

Instruments like drums, rattles, and jaw harps are routinely used. In medieval Rome, for example, women would drum and play tambourines during funerals of family members and later at the gravesites, until they were forbidden to do so by clerics and faced excommunication. Zimbabwean shamans use a thumb piano to summon ancestors to bring in animals for the hunt. Siberian shamans, when traveling along a road, will stop at burial sites and play their drums or jaw harps for the deceased. Some Tuvan shamans have special drumming techniques and rhythms for communicating with particular ancestors. The Nepalese ceremonialize the First Shaman with singing and drumming.

Ask each of the ancestors to give you a unique song for summoning. According to Celtic shaman Frank MacEowen, "The ancestors sing." In fact they seem to take great joy in passing their songs along to descendants. The songs used by a new Oroqen shaman, for instance, are those used by previous ancestor-shamans. Among Native-Americans, shamans may get their songs from ancestor-shamans in dreams or shamanic journeys. Nepalese shamans say that ancestors will respond to a special song. Sometimes an ancestor will give to a Vodou shaman a sacred song for singing directly into the body of a client. Guarani shamans are given special songs by their ancestors in dreams to use against evil spirits. Native-Americans in the Northwest say that after people die an ancestor will recognize them in the spirit world by the special songs they sing. Bushmen shamans get a personal song of a relative who just died, then use it to contact that particular ancestor for help in healing. The ancestor will then tell them how to see into the body of a client, what therapy to use, and so on.

You might also use a popular song which, you are sure, your ancestors would personally enjoy, such as the one they would love to sing or play during their earthly lives. My deceased father, for example, was stationed in the Caribbean during World War II and took a liking to Xavier Cugat's music, which he would play at home on our old phonograph. Think especially of a particular song that was popular, or that they especially liked, during their teenage years. We know that, during this life stage, music is especially important, and that an emotional resonance for a type of music that was highly popular then remains for a lifetime, say Ragtime for the American young of the early C20[th.]

Dance

Spirits, say the shamans, love to dance. Some shamans, in fact, find dancing indispensable for their work. According to African Zulu shaman Patience Koloko, "I have to dance and sing before I'm able to heal anybody." So incorporating a special dance into your ancestral honoring is a good thing to do. Euroamerican shaman Josie Raven-Wing, for example, holds dances for people to communicate with their ancestors. Ulchi shamans use dance to do the same. Vodou shamans in New Orleans hold public dances that include ancestral veneration. Yokuts dance at their ancestor-honoring ceremonies to have fun. For greater power, experienced shamans will invite the energy–"the spirit"–of the ancestors into the physical movements.

Any talk of ancestral dance must at least mention the Native-American Ghost Dance, a ceremony held to connect with the ancestors for protection against European colonizers. The Dance was so feared by U.S. officials that it led to the massacre in 1890 by the U.S. army at Wounded Knee in South Dakota, during which at least 150 Native-Americans were killed.

One idea is to learn the classical folk dances of your ancestors, like the Polka of the Polish and the Highland Dance of the Scots. You can do the dance while playing or listening to the appropriate ethnic music and wearing the period clothes you've made yourself.

So get down and boogie. As the chant of Buryat shamans goes:

> Till the sun sets beyond low hills
> we will thunder, we will dance!
> We'll bring to life the ancient ways
> of our forefathers as we dance!

Apologizing, Thanking, Forgiving

Shamans of yesterday and today have worked to keep their communities harmonious. But our relationships with certain ancestors may have been far less so. For this reason shamans have practiced "The Big Three Ceremonies," as I like to call them, to bring us back into spiritual resonance with the Old Ones: apology, thankfulness, and forgiveness. In fact as often happens today, scholarship is documenting the usefulness of shamanic practices, and these three ceremonies are no exception, having been found healthful in research by positive-psychologists. So, as you think about what ceremonies to do, you might place top priority on telling your Old Ones: I'm sorry; I thank you; I forgive you. These practices can bring a wealth of benefits to both you and your ancestors.

You might want to hold these three ceremonies before any others, because they can clear the air for future contacts. They can erase from consciousness any lingering issues that you and your ancestors may have had with each other. They can also cleanse from your *energy body*, aka energy field that permeates and surrounds the physical body, any darkness left over from relationships that went sour in physical reality. So if your family tree has grown so dysfunctional that you couldn't hold a reunion because nobody would come, think about doing the Big Three right now. Really.

Start by making a list of all your relevant ancestors. If you're an American who wants to hold these ceremonies for a grandparental ancestor, for extra juju you can do them on 8 September, Grandparents Day–a power time as it were.

Apology. Think of holding this ceremony first, since it puts the ancestor in a good mood. It shows that you come in good faith, with an honest heart, serious about wanting a harmonious relationship. It also makes them more open to your subsequent thanking and forgiving. The Ulchi, for example, ask their ancestors to forgive their mistakes. Buryat shamans hold a ceremony to apologize for all the disrespect their people have heaped upon the earth. Fijians hold one to request forgiveness for violating sacred obligations.

Next to the name of each Old One on your list, itemize all the particular ways you've disrespected them. Here are a few examples to get you started. You might say: I'm sorry for

> Missing your funeral
> Ignoring you for so long

Changing my name out of shame and spite
Writing off your wise advice
Failing to fulfill the potential you left me
Leaving my bedroom a mess
Acting like a 2-year old when I was 15
Saying mean things about you
Mistreating your other descendants
Dismissing you when you needed help.

Then apologize for each item aloud, if possible in front of a photo or effigy of the ancestor. You can also draw pictures representing the items. When finished, release your energetic attachment to the items by destroying them using your favorite elemental nature-spirit (by burning if it's Fire, by burying if it's Earth, and so on).

Thanksgiving. Does your lineage embarrass you? If so, this is not a good thing. According to Trinidadian author Wayne Trotman, "People who are ashamed of their heritage cannot be trusted." So, it may be wise to make a special effort to see the brighter side of your Old Ones.

In fact, this is what shamanic cultures do. Indigenous people have little if any sense of entitlement, instead being thankful for even the smallest things, and in particular for their ancestors. The Quiche, for example, hold fire ceremonies to thank the ancestors for their blessings. Korean and Japanese shamans say people need to show the ancestors gratitude. Fijians thank the ancestors with feasts upon the birth of a child and later at its death, for giving them the child and then taking it back. Vodou practitioners thank the ancestral world by publicly showing off their inherited talents, like a melodious singing voice or athletic prowess.

You might say: I thank you for

> Working two jobs so our family could make it
> Changing those countless diapers
> Reading me bedtime stories
> Telling me bedtime stories
> Teaching me how to defend myself
> Cooking my favorite dishes
> Always remembering my birthday
> Putting up with my weird boyfriend
> Driving me to concerts
> Restricting my TV viewing.

Then do the energetic release as above in the case of apology. The attitude of gratitude may get you everywhere with the ancestors.

If you're a Canadian or American, for extra juju you might do the gratitude ceremony on your respective national Thanksgiving day–a power time as it were. I personally thank my deceased Grandpa at that time for handing down to me his feisty independence. (When I was a kid, every Thanksgiving dinner turned into a battle royal over whether he, a Type 1 diabetic, should have dessert or not. He would instigate the dispute, then sit back to enjoy it. Phrases like blood sugar, insulin shock, and diabetic coma swirled around the room. When the dust had settled, the consensus was always: "Well, he can have a little." But after the table was cleared and the pumpkin pies were passed around, he would cut himself a big slice and then, just to show everybody that no one was going to tell him what to eat, top it off with a mountain of whipped cream. Despite his illness, for which the male life expectancy is 66 years, he lived to the age of 87, after years of being studied by medical researchers trying to figure out why he was still living.)

Forgiveness. Now the ancestors should be ready for your pardoning ceremony. They should be in a good-enough mood to listen to their own transgressions against you and then, you hope, accept your forgiveness. Vodou practitioners, for example, forgive the ancestors for disgracing the family name with scandals.

Don't be shy about doing this ceremony, especially if you live in a culture that says you must never speak ill of the deceased, which just represses any anger you may still harbor–not good for your soul. Too, the Old Ones remember quite well how they've hurt you. Scientists used to tell us that memory resided in the brain and so disappeared with brain-death, but now we know not only that memory is not "in" the brain at all, but even that it endures after brain death, as countless studies of NDEs have demonstrated. From my own NDE I can testify that, when I was out of my body, my memory was quite alive and well. Too, many NDErs go through an entire life review, sins and all. The evidence strongly suggests, then, that the ancestors remember clearly their earthly lives, warts included, and so they may even be grateful if you go out of your way to forgive them.

You might say: I forgive you for

> Telling me I'd never amount to anything
> Abusing me
> Being a deadbeat dad
> Refusing to let me have a BB gun
> Embarrassing me in front of my friends
> Leaving me out of your will
> Opening my mail

Ruining Christmas by knocking over the tree
Lacking the courage to teach me about sex
Favoring my siblings over me.

Then do the energetic release as above as in the cases of apology and thanksgiving.

Very important here is to forgive with compassion. Wishing them to feel even the slightest guilt will likely drive them away. So beforehand, for every item, dig into your own soul to find out how you may have occasioned their hurting you. Too, ask them what was going on in their mind when they did. In short, instead of belaboring your pain, understand theirs. This way you can avoid any ego-based "blame game" of self-righteousness. In fact your honest compassion may, with just a little luck, elicit their sympathy for the suffering they brought.

You may even be surprised that, instead of evoking ancestral self-defensiveness, your forgiveness causes relief and even joy that you've cleared away any guilt, shame, and remorse they were feeling. It also gives them a chance to apologize for their offenses. In fact, mediums report that many ancestors will say they are sorry right on the spot. Other ancestors may show up unexpectedly and specifically ask to be forgiven. This shows, as American mediums Joel Martin and Patricia Romanowski put it, that some ancestors "need us to help them . . . with . . . our . . . forgiveness."

Reconciliation, then, is likely to ensue. When I personally took a shamanic journey to forgive an ancestor, right away he ran up to me laughing and gave me a huge loving hug. I was taken aback and suddenly felt more whole. Tears flowed. Beautiful.

All three ceremonies heal both you and your ancestors. They repair your damaged soul. That is, apologizing relieves you of guilt and shame; thanking undermines your egoism—your habit of being a selfish little ingrate; and forgiving pulls you out of the muck of resentment. All three too, by clearing up unresolved issues with the recently deceased, can shorten your grieving time and so lower your risk of depression. Also, by shedding the burdens of the past, you can live more fully in the now, which is crucial for fulfilling your destiny.

All three ceremonies also repair the damaged souls of your ancestors. That is, the Old Ones will likely feel less wounded after your apologizing, more appreciated after your thanking, and less guilty after your forgiving. In short, their afterlives shine brighter. In fact, if they are stuck on the earthly plane because they are still holding on to their feelings of woundedness, under-appreciation, and guilt, then your ceremonies may in fact assist them in crossing over into the Light.

All three ceremonies, then, are effective tools for the spiritual advancement of both you and your ancestors. You can move on with your life and they can move on with their afterlives. If we stay mired in the past, we are unable to mature, whether in this life or the next—we stay babies. By taking care of unfinished business, the Big Three can unstick both the descendants and the ancestors. With respect to forgiveness, for example, as American medium John Holland put it, "When someone who passes asks for forgiveness and it's . . . given, it helps them progress on the other side."

That is, our connecting with ancestors fosters our collective destiny. Our lives and their afterlives are entangled. We all evolve by helping each other—sound familiar? According to

Jeffrey Wands, "their growth and ours remain intertwined because helping us down here is part of their growth up there— as we grow, so do they."

Like I said, *co-evolution.*

CHAPTER 5

Connecting in the Metaphysical Realm

Identifying an ancestor . . . has taken me to places I'd never have gone to before.

British comedian Jeremy Hardy

Now you have some specific practices in your ordinary realm for encouraging contact with the Old Ones. Shamanism also recognizes an array of ways in their nonordinary realm, the world of the spirits, for promoting connection. The Makuna people of the Amazon, for example, hold special ceremonies to take them into the ancestral domain.

Shamanic Journeys

You can make a spirit visit to your ancestors, immediate or remote ones, by way of the classic shamanic journey, or have a shaman do one for you or with you. Mapuche shamans, for example, go into an SSC for the sake of journeying to an ancestor for power to heal their people. Be ready for wonderful surprises. While on such a journey, for example, Scandanavian author Torstein Simonsen received an unknown surname of an ancestor which he later verified.

You'll likely contact healthy and helpful ancestors, but some are much less so, inhabiting a region with certain dangers, so you'll need to specify clearly that you only want to encounter benevolent ones. Shamans also stress that the journey needs to be done with the accompaniment of spirit helpers and with a focused objective, be it a simple "meet and greet" or a very specific request, say for a job. (Realize here, as the saying goes, that while all prayers are heard, only some are answered. The compassionate spirits give us what our souls need, not necessarily what our egos want.)

You can journey along paternal or maternal line. If you're a beginner, then starting with the line you feel closest to, and most comfortable with, may make some sense. Once you're experienced in the process, then you can shift to the other line, which is even more important. Why more important? Because you can learn much more. I've found a wealth of information by asking estranged ancestors a lot of difficult questions, such as: What went wrong with our relationship? What was the deep cause of the problem? What was my responsibility for the tension? How can I make it up to you now?

Is it better to contact immediate or remote ancestors? This is a complex question, so here are some considerations. With respect to immediate ancestors, on the one hand you may still have some emotional hang-ups, which make a clear and smooth journey difficult. You may be carrying along too much personal history, too much disturbing baggage. On the other hand, your knowledge of the ancestor may make for an easy trip and a lot of pertinent topics to talk about. Some historians, for example, in their search for the causes of events, use a simple rule–the "three-generation reach-back"–to get the greatest relevance, detail, and accuracy. This stretch of time is far enough back to find important roots, but not so far back as to find only trivial ones. Too, immediate ancestors may understand your contemporary problems better and feel your life situation more intimately, and so connect with you more closely, than remote ones.

With respect to remote ancestors, on the one hand you need to ask: Do they "have time" for me?–just do the math for the number of descendants they may feel responsible for. Assuming they do "have the time," you may need to send an especially strong signal to get their attention. On the other hand, Bwiti cultists, using the entheogenic iboga root in ceremony, are able to communicate with even the most remote of their ancestors. Too, it is said that remote ancestors have likely had "plenty of time" to process their own issues, and so have fewer self-regarding concerns, and greater wisdom and compassion, than immediate ones.

Two ways of journeying are possible. One, your helping spirits can decide on the specific time and place of the ancestor to be contacted, say 1850 Sophia in Bulgaria. Two, you or a shaman can decide. In either case, having a clear and specific itinerary–time and place locks–just prior to your journey is important for the success of your spirit-tracking.

Reconstructing Ancient Ceremony

Recovering olden ceremonies is an enjoyable way to access the ancestors in their realm. This practice is especially important for Euroamericans, whose ceremonial heritage has been repressed and largely gone missing and who are hungry for an authentic spirituality. Although growing numbers are saying they are "spiritual but not religious." many still feel spiritually homeless, having disconnected from their ancestral lands and traditions. They feel rootless and maybe even a little homesick, suffering from what might be called *ancestor-deficit disorder* that leaves them with a sense of loss.

Many of these spiritual refugees try to fill their hole in the soul by way of genealogical charts and so on, but these soulless attempts still leave them empty inside and longing for something deeper. Some try to copy Native-American practices, leading to some tension and distrust between the two ethnic groupings. Some Native-Americans even launch accusations of "culture-vultureing." Euroamericans are told to recover—or at least to reconstruct somehow—the sacred practices of their own traditions instead of "stealing" and "exploiting" those of others.

In fact they do sense some ancestral rumblings. I have a strong feeling that the old and forgotten practices are somehow embedded in our bones and can be recovered with just a little effort. During one of my shamanic ceremonies I instinctively felt that I should smudge around my body three times clockwise, and I spontaneously did so. It just felt right. Later I found out that the Tuvans, during one of their ceremonies, circle around special "shaman trees" three times clockwise. So I felt that somehow I had tapped into a kind of ancient shamanic residue. My ancestral memory was alive and well. Ancestral traditions, then, may be forgotten but not at all lost.

In fact we can recover these spiritual roots by digging deeply into the Land of the Deceased. Some reports say that Mapuche shamans, for example, are specifically tasked with recovery of ancestral practices.

So just ask the ancestors to bring to you the old practices. The Native-American Ghost Dancers, for example, journeyed into the ancestral realm to recover the old pre-contact traditions. Fijians say that the ancestors are enthusiastic and supportive when we try to revere the old ways—both the physical and the spiritual ones. So modern peoples, with ancestral help, can recover their own indigenous practices of old—Slavic, Norse, and the like—that have receded into the mists of time. By doing so, they will not have to rely on cultural appropriation—some would say expropriation—of those of other peoples.

There are added benefits. For the Matsigenka in Peru, ceremonial recovery helps the people "in keeping up traditions, and functions therefore in the interests of cultural continuity."

Here is one such journey I took to my Slavic ancestors. I asked, "Can you show me a ceremony for the spring equinox that will reflect the old ways but will also resonate with modern people?" They gave me this protocol:

Participants gather out in nature at dawn, each with a dish of food. They build a fire and then plant, around it in a big circle, eight tree seedlings, one for each cardinal and sub-cardinal direction, to symbolize the new life of spring. They then dance around the ring of seedlings four times, then sit down surrounding the fire. The dishes are then passed around, with each participant taking something from each dish. Then songs are sung. Then the children, symbolizing the new life of spring, entertain with acts they have created such as skits, stories, stand-up comedy, and the like.

Primitive potluck anyone? Entertainment provided.

Plant-Spirit Tripping

The ethnographic literature is replete with stories of indigenous shamans using entheogenic plants to go into an SSC in order to contact ancestors—the spirits of the plants serving as the shaman's allies. For example, Amazonian shamans use ayahuasca to connect with their Old Ones. According to ayahuascero Fernando Payaguaje, "I've had conversations with my dead relatives." Little wonder the plant is so often called the "vine of the dead."

Likewise, Fang tribalists in the Bwiti cult of Gabon drink a potion made from the iboga plant in a ceremony that takes them into a symbolic death-rebirth experience. The point is to "die" like the ancestors in order to talk with them in the spirit realm. Fijian shamans, for their part, give ceremonial participants a drink made from the sacred yaqona plant in order to set up a channel to the ancestors—"like dialing a telephone" as they put it. Koryak elders of Siberia also use a psychotropic plant, the mushroom *Amanita muscaria*, to communicate with the ancestors.

To shamans, a psychotropic plant is not a mere stationary botanical in the ground. It takes them on wild trips.

Walking About

We may also contact ancestors by making a special physical outing to obtain and learn about our special gift of power for our people. A popular example is the Native-American vision quest, during which the seekers enter an SSC allowing them to connect with the Old Ones in order to access that gift. Some Euroamericans too report conversing with an ancestor who appears to them in dreams during a vision quest. In a Japanese version of the practice, young boys enter the spirit world to be initiated by their ancestors into adulthood through a series of trials.

Aborigines have a like tradition. Eons ago, it is told, ancestral spirits moved through the land creating rivers, mountains, and so on, then became trees and stars and the like. So, particular objects of nature have special power because the energy of ancestor-creator spirits still resides in them. Adolescent males, then, go into the wilderness of the Outback in order to travel along these ancestral paths for as long as six months–taking a "walkabout." During their treks on these so-called "songlines," they are able to access the deposits of power left by the Old Ones.

Likewise the Norse tradition of going to a wild place and then "sitting-out" in an SSC is used to access the wisdom and power of the ancestors. A Scandanavian Sami shaman-ancestor, for example, who appeared to Torstein Simonsen, prompted him to do a sitting-out, during which he was given ancient songs known as *yoik*. The Q'ero people too travel along paths hosting shrines devoted to connecting with ancestral power. Huichols also find ancestral power on the landscape. They travel to their Wirikuta region, or "dancing patio" of the ancestors, where the sacred peyote cactus is found, then hold ceremonies inviting the ancestral spirits to join them. Like the Aborigines, they have a notion of songlines for connecting with the Old Ones. The ancestors do love those songs.

Psychopomp Work

Some ancestors have yet to cross over into the Light, and instead are stuck "between the worlds," between "earth and heaven" as it were. Classically the shaman has been the one who helps such unsettled ghosts work through their unresolved issues and then enter a state of peace. Unless this *psychopomping*, aka soul-guiding or soul-rescuing, is done, the ghosts may disrupt–haunt–us the living. This is not good. In contrast, if such souls are psychopomped, they may return to help the very people they were haunting.

You as a caring descendant may be tempted to do such work by yourself, but this is not advisable. Why? One, stuck ghosts inhabit a particular realm that has its dangers, so without the help of spirit allies whom you have cultivated over several years, journeys to that world can leave you unprotected. Two, as a descendant you are likely to still be emotionally involved with the stuck ancestors–namely stuck with your own unresolved issues–and so have trouble seeing things clearly. In short, this is a job for an experienced and more disinterested shaman.

So, you can ask a shaman to journey for you into the ancestral realm to psychopomp any stuck ancestors. Not only is this a compassionate way to contact your Old Ones, but the shaman may then be able to share with you some useful information about the challenges they faced previously in their earthly lives and currently in their nonearthly ones.

To sum up, shamans have devised a lot of specific practices to clear the portal between us and the Old Ones so we can establish contact. But how will you know if in fact you've connected? With experience, you'll start to sense a deep intimacy and benevolence. You'll start to feel a strong buzz–*an energetic resonance.*

The ancestors may then start to show up, in dramatic and surprising ways, in your life. How? Let me show you.

CHAPTER 6

Typical Manifestations

[A]ncestors . . . are very important. Compassionate spirits . . . have compassion for suffering beings in general. But ancestors tend to be the most compassionate toward their descendants.

Michael Harner, recipient of special honors by the American Anthropological Association for his pioneering work on shamanism

After using your set of shamanic practices, you may well find the ancestors manifesting in your life "unexpectedly." Yet such visitations are hardly a mere set of random occurrences. Rather, they appear to have some predictability. First, they seem to depend on certain operating principles, many of which can be manipulated by ancestors and descendants alike. As one of my shamanic teachers, Tom Brown, Jr., told me, "You're a conduit, but you're also a generator." Second, some types of manifestation are more common than others.

Conditionality

The reports above suggest that the likelihood of ancestral manifestation varies with certain operational principles. Shamans and researchers alike may want to test these hypotheses systematically in their work. To summarize and formalize:

{} *Crisis.* A situation worrisome or threatening to an ancestor or descendant, especially death, may well bring a manifestation.

{} *Group summoning.* Descendants who group together to call ancestors will be more successful than those who go it alone.

{} *Generational partiality.* Descendants who summon grandparental ancestors are most likely to score an encounter.

{} *Specific summoning.* When a particular ancestor is beckoned by a descendant, an appearance is more likely.

{} *Name invoking.* Descendants who avoid name silence and call an ancestor's name aloud are more likely to have an encounter.

{} *Triggering.* The more a descendant takes advantage of positive triggers and avoids negative ones, the more likely a manifestation.

{} *Familiarizing.* The more a descendant takes advantage of the familiarizing effect and avoids the defamiliarizing one, the more likely a manifestation.

{} *Confidence.* The more a descendant is convinced an encounter will happen, the greater its likelihood.

{} *Intimacy.* The stronger the emotional connection between ancestor and descendant, the more likely the ancestor will show up.

{} *Persistence.* A descendant who shows resolve over time in trying to induce a manifestation will more likely experience one.

{} *Psychic competence.* The greater the psychic openness and ability of the descendant, the more likely an ancestor will manifest.

American psychic Margaret Wendt, for example, reported several meetings with her beloved ancestral grandfather after many specific and urgent summons. So, when conditions like these prevail, don't be surprised if the Old Ones show up. Blood, we might say, is thicker than death.

We've touched on some ways that ancestors may manifest in the lives of shamans and their clients. But it's worth singling out the four most common scenarios whereby they show up in most people's lives: death visitations, ceremonial arrivals, incarnations, and dreams. These four are worth focusing and elaborating on, since they are found across the world and over the millennia. Too, greater detail will allow us to recognize them more easily for what they are, so we won't be confused or frightened or tempted to write them off as fantasy or hallucination.

Death Visitations

Likely the most common form is the death visitation, a happening fully documented in some excellent books and TV series. These appearances take two forms: (1) ancestors appear to a living descendant right after their deaths, or (2) dying descendants receive a visit from an ancestor, often right at their deathbeds.

The first form is found worldwide, and has been shown to occur independent of age, sex, religion, and other features. In Polynesia, for example, ancestors will appear to a family member right after their deaths. This kind of visitation often occurs even though the living descendants do not know that the ancestor has died. Soon after the visit, though, they hear the news. The contacts may come in many forms, such as falling photos, radio voices, phone calls, computer screen images, fragrances of tobacco smoke or flowers associated with the ancestor, synchronicities, and so on. Deceased loved ones have a lot of ways to say Goodbye.

The second form is also common. Maybe you've heard of people who were dying, and before the final moment exclaimed that they had just received a visit from an ancestor. Clearly the Old One is trying to comfort the descendants on their deathbeds and to welcome them to the other side–acting as a sort of psychopomp to ease the transition from one life to the next. Sometimes the ancestor and dying descendant engage in a two-way conversation. Nurses, hospice workers, and other caregivers for the dying are familiar with such a happening, but regrettably many dismiss it as patient hallucination. Usually, though, the visitation is a fact-based omen that the descendants will expire shortly. After the visit, many patients report a decline of pain and depression, and claim a willingness to leave this life, even expressing peace and joy about the prospect.

As the descendant is passing away, the ancestor–often a grandparent–may even be seen by bedside observers to be psychopomping the soul to the other side. "I could psychically see," said American medium Echo Bodine about her friend's death, "his soul come out of his body and take his [deceased] parents' hands." In another case involving her own father, she saw her "grandma hovering over dad . . . prior to his passing . . . and when he left his body, she took him immediately to the other side."

A variation on the second form is the NDE, during which experiencers meet ancestral spirits who tell them, "You need to go back, it's not your time." Death, then, seems to be a common encounter moment, be it the "real deal" or a "dry run."

Death visitations bring solace to the living. But more than that, they point to postmortem survivability. As one previously skeptical descendant, American psychic Margaret Wendt, put it after a family member's death, "I know we don't die, I saw my [deceased] grandfather."

Ceremonial Arrivals

Ancestors like to make visual appearances, aka apparitions and waking visions, in dramatic ways. Among the Yakut, for example, ancestors may show up in full-bodied form, commonly wearing traditional clothes.

Often the appearances occur during ceremonies honoring the Old Ones. In Japan, for example, ancestral spirits visit villages, shrines, and individual descendants during festivals in order to make their desires known, and may even possess the celebrant-shaman who tells participants what the visitors from the other side desire. The participants may even communicate directly with the ancestors who show up. Tuvan ancestors also appear during shamanic ceremonies. Zapotec ones return to earth during the Day of the Dead festival in Mexico to commune with the living and check on their welfare. Dukhan shamans find their ancestor-shamans showing up during ceremonies. Aborigines, too, often see their ancestors in various ways during ceremonies of song and dance in their honor. During the Mandan Sun Dance in North America, ancestors may arrive to dance with their descendants. So, if you should host such a song and dance ceremony, don't be surprised if you wind up with a Grateful Dead concert in your own backyard!

Sometimes, though, the ancestors appear to descendants not directly but indirectly through an apparition seen by a medium doing a connection ceremony in physical reality. The literature on mediums who link descendants on earth with their ancestral visitors from the spirit world is vast.

Incarnations

Indigenous people often sense the presence of ancestors in material things. The Makuna, for example, see natural objects like rivers and mountains as personifications of their ancestors. Other peoples see their Old Ones possessing the bodies of wild animals, such as peccaries and sharks. Still others view their ceremonial musical instruments as being inhabited by ancestral clan spirits. The indigenes of Easter Island see their Moai statues as being alive with the spirits of ancestors.

The physical bodies of descendants may be possessed, voluntarily or involuntarily, by their ancestors. In Polynesia, the Old Ones may possess descendants and speak through them. I once had a first-hand experience of such a happening. I was talking face-to-face with a friend whose father, whom I knew well, had just passed away. Suddenly my friend's face morphed into the face of his father and stayed that way for several seconds. This type of possession is not difficult, due to the similar energetic signatures of ancestor and descendant. I later found out the technical term for this happening: *transfiguration*.

The deceased may also possess a shaman or medium asked by a client-descendant to contact that soul. According to the report of one such client, Margaret Wendt, the medium spoke in a voice that "was her grandfather's" and took "on her grandfather's countenance."

Service as we Sleep

Shamans might say that if you want your ancestors to show up, especially immediate ones, go to sleep. Professional dream researchers have documented such happenings for many decades. But this is hardly news to indigenous cultures, like that of the Aborigines. Zulu descendants are even told by an ancestor in dreams exactly who is going to live and die so they can make appropriate plans.

If you're unsure a dream is a visitation by an ancestor, here's a checklist to use. Such dreams are likely to be *clear* (like being awake or having a waking vision), *vivid* (intense, hyper-real, larger than life), *familiar* (the visitor being known or recognizable as an ancestor), *powerful* (strongly energetic), *mysterious* (eerie, wondrous), *meaningful* (significant, purposeful, applicable to daily life), *symbolic* (featuring personally important signs), *moving* (emotionally resonant), *memorable* (recallable in full detail, hard to forget), *predictive* (telling of future events), *verifiable* (testable against future information), often quite *helpful* (contributing to your wellbeing), and sometimes *repeated* (occurring more than once with the same message within a short period). The Iroquois regard such dreams as "Big Dreams" requiring special attention with respect to interpretation and follow-up action, otherwise unfortunate consequences may ensue.

Often descendants dream of an ancestor telling them things they were unaware of. Later the information is verified. Not surprisingly such a dream will often occur right after the deaths of family members, who are letting the descendant know that they are alive and well–they just went into another realm. These dreams happen especially if the deaths themselves were unknown by the descendants.

CHAPTER 7

All Wine and Roses?

None of us can boast about the morality of our ancestors. The record does not show that Adam and Eve were ever married.

American editor E. W. Howe

If you're thinking that your ancestors are largely benevolent, you're likely right, but this notion can blind us to the fact that holding an open house for the Old Ones may not be good for you and me. Fijians, for example, say that ancestors can bring both blessings and burdens, both help and harm, to our everyday lives. Chepang shamans in Nepal report that the ancestors they encounter in their spirit journeys may not be very friendly. The ancestors, then, may be alive but not necessarily well, so we cannot afford to be indiscriminate.

But why even deal with this Dark Side of our ancestors? Some mediums, for example, steadfastly refuse to even deal with any ancestral negativity. (If you've ever had a hair-raising experience with a nasty spirit, you understand why and even sympathize.)

So why not just live and let live, so to speak? Do you remember the studies I described above about the ancestor effect? Now let me tell you the rest of the story The researchers found that the students scored higher on the tests *even when they remembered the negative aspects of their ancestors*. Did the students want to reverse their negative heritage by showing that "my ancestral line can do better than this"? Were they defiantly showing that they would not be burdened by their dark heritage? We don't know. Whatever the reasons, my own mantra is that it's always good to look truth straight in the face, even when it's about the spoiled fruit on our family tree. The truth may hurt but in the long run it's therapeutic.

Hooligan Reports

Some bureaucratic religions almost automatically label ghosts as "demons" or some variant thereof–society's metaphysical outlaws. Indigenous cultures, while not going that far at all, do recognize that hostile ancestors can bring bad luck in many forms, such as illnesses, accidents, and familial strife. The Ulchi put it bluntly: The ancestors "sometimes behave like hooligans."

People who die with unresolved issues may stick around the earthly plane and cause a variety of physical and psychological problems for the living. Such Old Ones are stuck in the same state in which they died, namely they stop evolving. Buryat culture, for instance, especially fears the ancestors who died a violent death, since they become angry ghosts.

They may come into our world, for example, seeking revenge for our misdeeds. For this reason in ancient Greece, a deceased spirit was thought to be capable of inflicting disease on family survivors. The ancient Romans too said that, if the Old Ones are not respected, they could trouble the living. Koreans today express fear of "spiteful" ancestors In many African cultures, upset ancestors can withhold help and guidance from descendants and even act antagonistically. Hoodoo practitioners have found that spiteful ancestors may deliberately scare their descendants with apparitions or slaps in the face. In Fiji, a story asserts that a man who publicly denied his misdeeds was punished by his ancestors with the death of his son. In Russian folklore, if descendants displease the clan "Grandfather," He may start throwing things around the house and even burn it down.

Involuntary possession of descendants by the Old Ones may happen more often than we think. In Melanesia, a hooligan ancestral ghost may enter the bodies of descendants, causing them to quiver and shake all over. Ancestors who were overprotective parents may possess a living child because they think they know what's best for their progeny. A "familist" or "clannist" ancestor may possess descendants to keep them in line with the ideals of the lineage. Other ancestors may possess a descendant because they refuse to accept their own deaths and want to live on in the physical realm.

Soul-theft is another form of hooliganism. In Siberia an ancestor may be angry about a descendant's behavior that caused disrespect for the lineage of the family or clan. In such cases the Khanty make great efforts to mollify the ancestor, otherwise their souls may be stolen, which then need to be retrieved by a shaman by way of bribing or battling the offender in the spirit world. The Inuit too report that a lonely and lovesick ancestor may steal the soul of a living descendant.

Yet we need to think twice before automatically playing judge, jury, and executioner of apparent hooligans. Here's an example. The Washo people of California discourage parents from physically punishing their children, otherwise the ancestors may kill the punished child, namely their descendant. This case sounds like simple and nasty—not to mention mysterious—ancestral vengeance. But look at it from the viewpoint of the deceased. They get a "threefer," aka 3 for the price of 1: (1) they fulfill their duty as "elders" and "parents" to discipline their abusive descendant-children; (2) they save their beloved descendant-grandchild from further physical pain; and (3) they get to enjoy the company of this grandchild in their afterlives. In Fiji too it is said that such *apparently* bad outcomes need to be seen in the broader light of the ancestors. American genealogist Laurence Overmire agrees, pointing out that we need to take a wider view of the consequences of ancestral disturbances: "If you can make your ancestors real for yourself . . . you will see yourself in the Big Picture."

Grave Grievances

Issues surrounding burials and gravesites often appear in hooligan reports. Ancestors may come in our dreams to chide us about not caring for their graves. This is why, for example, the Chinese hold a special cleansing ceremony called "Tomb Sweeping." Central Asian shamans look after ancestral graves and say prayers and leave offerings at the sites. In parts of ancient Europe, burial sites hosted curse inscriptions threatening desecrators with dire consequences. The Ewe-speaking people of West Africa seek the good will of their ancestors by pouring wine and beer on their graves. Like I said, don't forget the booze.

Native-Americans are adamant about protecting their burial grounds, otherwise the ancestors can become really nasty if the sites are abused. The victims of ancestral wrath may include not only descendants but also others who disrespect the gravesites, such as colonizers, as well as *their* descendants. As Suquamish Chief Seattle put it, "To us, the ashes of our ancestors are sacred and their resting place is hallowed ground." When burial bones are desecrated, the deceased may well go on the warpath.

In ancient Germany, ancestors who were not given a proper burial ceremony were seen as a threat to their descendants. In parts of England it is said that, if ancestors want their skulls buried inside the walls of their houses but the wish is denied, they will appear to descendants as screaming skulls and cause bad luck, including destruction of the houses and deaths of the residents. If the wish is fulfilled, the screaming and other maladies will stop, but resume if the skulls are removed.

Forget Me Not

The Khanty warn, "Those who do not love the ancestors, maybe it will be bad for them." A descendant who neglects the ancestors may make them displeased. In Fiji an ancestor may punish descendants if they disrespect tradition by treating it as no longer relevant. In Korea neglected ancestors can cause problems, so shamans go to great lengths to recite the individual names of all relevant ancestors during ceremonies. In Okinawa, ancestors may be upset about neglect by a descendant, say for not passing on their name to the newborn.

To Polynesians the ancestors, if not remembered, can become pathetic, homeless, wandering ghosts. In Japan, ancestors who are not honored may cause their descendants bad luck. Okinawan shamans often attribute bad luck to insufficient honoring of the Old Ones. In the Hawaiian tradition, ancestors who are not "fed" may recede far beyond a descendant's call, and may punish a descendant with sickness for violating ancestral prohibitions. In India, ancestors who are angry about being denied food and other offerings, or about being denied requests in dreams for help in transiting to the other side, are said by shamans to inflict on descendants a variety of ills. During the Mexican Day of the Dead, while sharing stories about the deceased, participants take care that no soul is neglected lest it get angry.

Dark Energy

Ancestors who are stuck on the earthly plane with unresolved issues carry dark energy, and shamans, who can sense this energy, know that serious problems arise when these ghosts start clinging to their descendants. Hoodoo practitioners, for example, report that some ancestors refuse to let go of the ones they love and left behind, with unfortunate consequences for the survivors. Such ancestors who benefit themselves at the expense of descendants have rightly been labeled spiritual parasites.

Recall here that both the deceased and the descendant have energy bodies, aka energy fields, which while distinct have similar energy signatures. Such fields have been well known to ancient and modern peoples alike, especially shamans. According to ethnographic studies, they are explicitly recognized in at least 100 cultures. But as American researcher Christopher Bache noted, "[F]ields are by nature porous." This means that energy bodies can penetrate each other, which is not good if they are covered with dark energy. Also they have the property of electromagnetism, which as we know can carry information, as in radio waves. This explains why powerful ghosts are able to operate almost any type of electrical appliance you can imagine, even when it's unplugged or lacking batteries. It may also explain why sometimes we get bizarre thoughts that seem to come out of nowhere.

Why is this important? Picture a ghost with a severe psychological problem, say compulsive hand washing. Some reports tell of such ancestors attaching themselves to descendants, thereby causing their own psychological disturbance to appear in the latter. How so? The ghost's electromagnetic energy field, carrying that malady, may enter into the porous energy field of the descendant, making the disruption materialize. This is easy for an ancestral ghost to do. Its field is likely stronger than the descendant's because it is unencumbered by a clunky physical body. Also, the two energy fields have similar energetic signatures and therefore resonate easily. Such an effect is most likely if the energy body of the ancestor is especially powerful and focused but that of the descendant is weak and scattered. For these reasons I've heard a number of my shamanic teachers tell me, in one way or another, to keep my energy field healthy. One put it especially well: "Practice *energy hygiene*!"

Among the Nage of Indonesia, for example, an ancestor may attach to living descendants and make them sick. Hoodoo practitioners say that ancestors may cling too closely to living descendants, causing serious problems. In Mexico a common shamanic practice is the healing of victims of ghostly dark energy, the so-called *mal aire* ("bad air"), aka ghost sickness, by means of a *limpia*, aka cleansing, ceremony. Ancient Greeks likewise feared the *miasma*, a heavy, depleting, corrupting, and polluting vapor caused by contact with a corpse that could bring disease to the surviving family unless a purification rite was held. Some Native-Americans too believe that recently deceased ancestors who stay next to their corpses can cause such a sickness in survivors. In Korea, a survivor who contacts the souls of deceased but troubled family members after their deaths may be beset by illness and other afflictions. Modern psychic Jeffrey Wands too notes the "bad air" of undesirable ancestral presence: "[T]heir negative energy can make life difficult for those left behind." British medium Gordon Smith also sees some survivors covered by a "heavy emotional blanket that is both weighing them down and blocking out the light that is there to be seen."

Might this kind of generational transmission be the reason why people say, "Oh, that problem just runs in the family"? But to what extent is *genetic* inheritance *not* responsible for such behaviors? To what extent is environmental learning *not* responsible for them either? Maybe, in short, it is *neither* nature *nor* nurture. Maybe, just maybe, we should look to the specters.

Welcome to My World?

Some reports say that the deceased may miss their family survivors so much that they even try to drag them into their afterworld. Such ancestors, not accepting their departure from earthly life, refuse to leave the still living and cling to them with negative consequences. A Cuban Santeria shaman, for example, will say that when ancestors see their descendants in pain, they may try to relieve it by bringing them into the spirit world. A Zapotec story tells of a deceased girl who held on to her surviving sister so tightly that the sister was walking through life like a "zombie." The ghost wanted her sister to join her and so was "pulling her into the next world."

For Polynesians too, after a death in a marriage, the deceased may try to pull the surviving spouse into its new home, causing soul-loss and even imminent death. Among the Native-American Salish, the newly deceased may hang around their old habitats trying to get their descendants' souls to join them, and may even cause the survivors to lose their property, thereby pushing them into poverty and despair and so into suicidality. The Bushmen too say that some ancestors cause sickness and death in family survivors so that those they miss so much can join them in the afterlife.

Cursed Lineages

There's more. The cursing of descendants by ancestors is not unknown. In a report about the Bushmen, for example, a deceased uncle cursed his living nephew for treating the ancestor's living brother badly.

In fact the attribution of maladies to malevolent transmission down a whole ancestral line can be found in a number of indigenous cultures. In Fiji, for example, an entire lineage may be cursed somehow, either deliberately or inadvertently. In the Himalayas, ancestors may curse a descendant for breaking a promise to honor them with spirit plates, for polluting or abandoning their gravesites, and so on, and the misfortunes may be passed down through the generations. Such curses may cause descendants to suffer co-morbid maladies like addiction.

Someone may be born, then, into some kind of trouble that has cascaded down to them from an ancestral line. For example, some indigenous cultures say that descendants of a sorcerer may suffer because of their ancestor's misdeeds. That is, spiritual pathologies may be transmitted from one generation to the next.

Some shamans, then, speak of a sort of miasma that is "passed down in the ancestral DNA of a person's spiritual, emotional, and physical energetic matrix," an imbalance in an energy body that can interrupt or corrupt one's natural healing ability. This is a spiritual sickness, an energetic disturbance passed down from generation to generation, springing from violation of taboos in the past or other causes. Still other practitioners like Rachel Stavis speak of ancestral curses being passed down by way of "spiritual DNA" from generation to generation.

We can find, in popular culture today, stories about ancestral curses, such as the one described in the documentary film *Horse Boy*. In 2007 an American couple, Rupert and Kristin Isaacson, traveled to Mongolia to enlist the help of shamans for their autistic son Rowan. The shamans sensed that some dark energy had entered Kristin's womb when she was pregnant, and they also saw an ancestral spirit who was pulling on Rowan's soul, an effort that was having negative effects on the boy. The spirit was a woman in Kristin's lineage who was behaving like a psychic with certain powers but who was also mentally unstable. Kristin felt that the woman might be her grandmother who had suffered from mental illness and who had been institutionalized after her own 8-year-old son was killed in a car accident. The shamans then held ceremonies for Rowan, which healed most of the boy's symptoms. Kristin then had a vivid dream in which her grandmother appeared joyous, as if she had finally let go of her living grandson and been healed.

In one of my own cases, a female client with a mental disturbance had been cursed by a likewise mentally disturbed female ancestor with miserably low self-esteem. The ancestor could not bear the idea of her descendants singling her out as a sort of "Crazy Aunt Sally," so she made sure that her female descendants would also suffer from that mental disturbance and hopefully would say instead, "It just runs in the family," thereby blaming it on genetic inheritance. What is interesting about such cases is that the victimized clients present with statements like "Our family must be cursed!" They say this half-jokingly, but also half-seriously, intuiting that deep-down they are healthy and that the problem stems from some non-personal source.

A whole ancestral line, moreover, may be cursed by entities *outside* of it. Almost everyone has heard stories, true or not, about archeologists and thieves—as well as their descendants—being cursed after disturbing the tombs of Egyptian pharaohs or the burial grounds of Native-Americans. Too, the descendants of an ethnic group, say the Turks, whose ancestors mistreated another group, say the Armenians, may find that their land has been cursed by that other group's ancestral spirits. They are now, literally, paying the price "for the sins of their fathers." That is, your ancestral line may have been cursed by another people who were abused by your own ancestors. In such cases a shaman may be called in to urge "peace talks" between the two "nations" in order to resolve the grievances and so reverse the curse.

An outside curse of a lineage may have come from a distant family trauma that opened the door to an attachment by a malevolent spirit. The spirit then continues its attachment from generation to generation through the mother in utero.

In one of my own cases, I was asked by a client to see if her lineage was somehow cursed. I took a shamanic journey and saw, four generations back in the U.S. South, two drunk men sitting around a campfire by a lake and blaming one of my client's ancestors for a financial loss he had caused them. Suddenly I saw a pregnant woman walking by the lake. The two men, recognizing her as the daughter of the man who had aggrieved them and seeking revenge, conjured up a dark entity that then used the campfire flames to curse the man's lineage, starting with his daughter and his to-be-born grandchild, with similar financial losses. At that point in my journey, I called on a helping spirit, a power animal, who scooped up water from the lake and doused the campfire, and then appeared above my client flapping its wings and saying, "Stay cool." Then it flew through the ancestral line, releasing the blessings that had been blocked by the curse and dropping blessings into the future. I saw the curse dissipating as it flew along the line. After my journey the client told me that, three generations back, a group of Ku Klux Klansmen had come to the house of one of her ancestors, burning a cross in his yard and then burning down the house itself.

So before we start blaming our ancestors for our misfortunes, we might do well to realize that they may have been cursed by their own ancestors or someone else, which in turn brought that bad luck to us. As American shaman Lisa Gunshore put it, some ancestors "were influenced in their life choices by things beyond their control." Like I said: Forgive.

The reports are also urging us to ask: Will our behavior today cause our descendants to be cursed tomorrow? Worth thinking about.

Preventive Measures

The shaman takes the hooliganism of ancestors seriously, since meddling with descendants can interfere with their destinies. Over the millennia, therefore, a variety of ways have been developed to protect us. For example, practitioners know that they themselves can be protected against malevolent spirits with the help of their own shaman-ancestors. They'll say that you too have available powerful shielding by compassionate ancestors, as well as other helping spirits, and they may hold a special protection ceremony for you and other potential victims. Mapuche shamans, for example, make ceremonial offerings to placate any disgruntled ancestors.

Among indigenous peoples, in fact, the ancestor-derived malady is so well-known that preventive measures may be taken right after a family member's death. Some Native-Americans, for example, bury their deceased on the same day as the death to reduce the amount of time they have to spend with the body. Others take full advantage of what I call the *defamiliarizing effect*, namely repelling undesired ancestors from a scene by making it unrecognizable and uncomfortable. The Inuit, for example, practice a ritual of wearing new clothes so that the deceased, if angry, will not recognize them and attack. The Korean shaman during funeral ceremonies makes sure the deceased will find their way to the afterlife so they will not bring misfortune to survivors. During the ceremonies, the shaman acts as a medium relaying any grievances of the deceased to survivors so that the souls will not stick around and wreak havoc out of revenge. In some parts of the U.S. South, survivors of a recent death in the family cover all mirrors with a black cloth to prevent the new ancestor from peering at them through the glass.

Name silence is a surprisingly common strategy. In Mongolia, for example, speaking the disgruntled deceased's name is avoided since this may call the soul back from the afterlife and encourage it to stick around the earthly plane. Native-Americans are known to follow the same prescription. An Inuit community may refrain from using the name of some ancestors lest they steal the souls of descendants. The Yokuts may even take new names for themselves that are different from those of the deceased.

Indigenous cultures also take measures to deal with the dwellings where death occurred. As paranormal investigator Karen Stevens put it, "Some ghosts linger in their former homes . . . because they enjoyed [them] . . . so much that they can't bear to leave." The Kulina people of Brazil abandon their whole village for weeks until the deceased have realized they've passed, at which time a shaman sings songs that conduct the souls to the afterlife. In some cultures, right after a death in a house, its residents keep the doors and windows open to ease the soul's departure. In New Zealand, the Maori stomp through the home to drive away the energy of the recently deceased relative, thereby keeping the soul at a respectful distance. Some Native-Americans simply abandon a house after a death and move to a new one. Others burn it, and where the new house is built, they burn poisonous plants around it in a smudging ceremony to repel the ghostly relative. Mexican shamans too will smudge a house after a death to cleanse it of the ancestor's energy. An Inuit shaman may swing a drumstick around it to remove any ancestral attachment. Ancient Romans purified it after the funeral, possibly employing a professional to do the job. Some modern mediums advise that everything be moved around inside the structure so the distraught spirit, seeking out the familiar, will no longer feel at home and so move on.

Getting rid of the deceased's possessions, which may bring a ghost sickness, is another strategy. Polynesians, for example, in order to prevent unwanted happenings due to a clinging ghost, may burn the clothes of the deceased. Gypsies too will burn a deceased's possessions so the soul does not stay attached to the earthly realm but instead moves on. Among the Lakota, the family releases the deceased from the earthly plane by giving away all of his or her possessions to the community. The Salish too, in order to prevent an ancestor from making survivors want to die so as to bring them into the afterlife, rid themselves of the deceased's belongings as soon as possible. Yokuts bury the possessions during the funeral ceremony and tell the deceased to go back to the Place of Peace: "Don't bother anyone, don't look back at your family, go home!" Ancient Europeans erected iron fences around gravesites to prevent the deceased from disturbing the living.

Negative triggers are also used. Some Inuit, for example, sprinkle human urine around the dwelling of a recently deceased ancestor. Such possibilities are endless. For example, a friend of mine despises Brussels sprouts, calling them "mutant cabbages." Should he turn out to be a hooligan ancestor, his descendants might grow the little mutants all around their property to keep him away.

Countering Vinegar and Weeds

Shamans, with the help of their spirit allies, assist descendant-victims of dysfunctional family members of the ancestral kind with proactive measures. They confront directly such "wrong-doers who need to be pacified and appeased," as Ildiko Beller-Hann called them. That is, they work to transmute the vinegar and weeds back into wine and roses.

When Korean shamans, for example, see an illness caused by a disgruntled ancestor, they drive out the malady by swinging a sword around the client in order to cut off the ancestor's energetic bonds. Mexican-American shamans use a similar technique to sever the disorder from the client. A Tuvan shaman may call out an ancestor of clients in order to remove a curse. In Egypt a ceremony of reconciliation is held to put an end to sicknesses and nightmares caused by hooligan ancestors. Some modern shamans journey to the cursors and negotiate with them to pull out the life force from the hex.

We can find a wealth of other examples. In Bali it is said that ancestors will cause mischief and harm if not regularly acknowledged with offerings, such as their favorite food. When maladies occur, a shaman is called in to recommend a ceremonial treatment, including a list of offerings to be made. A Santeria shaman may be summoned by clients in order to enlist their benevolent ancestors for healing the misfortunes caused by their malevolent ones and for future protection.

A hooligan ancestor may even take away the helping spirit of descendants, leaving them distraught. In such cases, shamans will advise some kind of power- or soul-retrieval ceremony, such as a journey to the spirit world and back again. Salish shamans, for example, in order to prevent a client-victim from suffering and dying, will hold a retrieval ceremony of this sort, traveling in a "spirit boat" to the afterlife realm and back.

Shamans can also heal the wounds of a miscreant ancestor by using their psi skills of telepathy, clairvoyance, and so on, and by so doing heal their victimized client as a result. In a word, they heal the hooligan and the client at the same time—they get a twofer. Here is a case from my own practice. A client with agoraphobia was healed after my helping spirits and I healed her female ancestor who was suffering from agoraphobia herself and who was clinging to her descendant. How so? My spiritual team took a shamanic journey and coaxed this ancestor into a shopping mall and gently lowered her anxiety. Today my client, while not exactly a shopaholic, is no longer a recluse either.

At times an outright removal of some kind from the scene may be necessary. To the Ulchi, for example, ancestors who committed murder or suicide are especially likely to bring harm to living descendants, and so a special clearing ceremony may be held. During certain ceremonies in ancient Rome, the head of a family addressed malevolent ancestors and asked for their blessings. The family head also made woolen dolls or bark masks representing the family members, then hung them from tree branches and asked any ancestors bent on harm to accept the effigies as substitutes for those family members. Amulets, incantations, and spells were also used. During one special ceremony, malevolent ancestors were cleared from homes by way of food offerings for these "hungry ghosts." Likewise, during a special Japanese festival, malevolent ancestors are led out of the community with positive triggers like food and dancing.

In especially difficult cases, shamans may have to reverse the malady by sending the negative energy back to the perpetrator. At other times they may have to engage in outright battle with the hooligans. A Bushmen shaman, for example, may have to wrestle with the ancestors who, by causing sickness and death, are trying to get their living descendants to join them in the afterlife

All these reports are telling us to steer clear of trusting ancestors uncritically. Some of them were less than spiritually healthy during their earthly lives and took their problems into the beyond, so we need discernment. You don't want your *danse celebrante* turning into a *danse macabre*. This is why we don't worship them.

Shamans know this well. In fact, experienced ones have a whole box of tools to protect you and will gladly serve as your ghostbuster if need be. So, who ya gonna call?

Chapter 8

Outcome Data

We bring with us the spirits of our ancestors.
We are haunted by their demons and protected
by their deities.

American writer William Ritter

We've seen that we meet up with our ancestors in our world and in theirs. Which of the two ways is more common, and specifically what happens in each? We've also seen that while some ancestors bring blessings, others bring misfortunes. In which worlds do each of these outcomes occur most often and how so in each?

Analysis

I made a rough, admittedly non-randomized, expedient-sample survey of reports of ancestral manifestations from the literature on indigenous cultures mentioned above, with special attention to shamanic and related practices. From this material I estimated the number of direct encounters between ancestors and descendants, as well as indirect ones involving shamans as well as mediums and related practitioners. Many of the encounters arose out of deliberate practices like healing, divination, celebration, protection, and so on, while others just occurred serendipitously, including synchronicities and cross-correspondences involving well-known details about an ancestor's biography and habits. Both positive and negative outcomes were considered.

I do not offer exact numbers, due to the sparseness and vagueness of some reports and so the possibility of inaccurate estimates. This summary, then, should be taken only as generalization, not strict quantitfication. Too, while it is global and cross-cultural and so includes a large number and variety of cases, no claim at all is made for comprehensiveness or perfect representativeness. It does, though, offer newcomers to ancestral study a broad overview, as well the relative emphasis they might want to put on any particular manifestation.

I grouped the encounters first into those occurring in ordinary, physical reality, and second into those occurring in nonordinary, metaphysical reality.

From Their World to Ours

In the words of American filmmaker Raquel Cepeda, "When we illuminate the road back to our ancestors, they have a way of . . . manifesting themselves . . . physically." Exactly. We can note here at the outset that the reports reveal the ancestors manifesting in our physical world more than twice as often as in their metaphysical one. This is understandable if we realize that ancestral souls, their energy bodies freed from their clunky physical ones, may well have the power to easily part the curtain separating their world from ours. Most living descendants, on the other hand, seem to lack that power. So, the claim that the ancestors are standing right next to us as we watch TV and cook dinner does in fact tap into a reality. The so-called dearly departed are not as apart as we think.

So let's look at these appearances in our everyday physical reality. Note here that I deliberately omitted the many reports of deathbed visitations–either to our deathbeds or from theirs–which I've described above. I also excluded reports by professional mediums who bring messages from immediate ancestors to survivors. These accounts would bolster the assertion above that we are much more likely to encounter ancestors in our reality than in theirs.

When the ancestors come into our world, what happens? Rather shocking is that the most frequent outcome, again excluding deathbed and medium visitations, is not good for you and me. This is the case in slightly over half of the total appearances in our reality. Psychological maladies, especially stress and anxiety in general and phobia and related disturbances in particular, make up almost one-fifth of such cases. We then find strings of bad luck and physical illnesses accounting for about one-tenth each, followed by material damage and death about equally distributed in another one-tenth or so. Medical practitioners take note: The malady you are diagnosing and treating may not be helped at all by PET scans, talk therapy, psychopharmacology, or any other physical-realm modality. Shamans know this well.

On a lighter note, the other half of appearances in our physical reality are benevolent. Most frequent are useful messages, whether spontaneous or solicited, and either directly transmitted by contact with effigies and funerary remains and gravesites, or indirectly relayed by shamans and related practitioners. Such information transfer occurred in about one-fifth of the cases. To these we can add communication by means of nature signs as well as voices–another one-twentieth. Ancestors do love to talk. Waking visions are also common, accounting for about one-eighth, and are reported occurring most often during shamanic ceremonies of some kind. So, if you want that special "paranormal caught on camera" shot, ask a shaman to start dancing. Filling out the count are ancestral embodiments in a person, namely merging, possession, and transfiguration, and healings of self or others, in the remaining one-tenth of cases.

From Our World to Theirs

Now let's look at experiences of ancestors in their metaphysical reality. That is, when we are able to transcend the physical by ourselves or through a shaman or related practitioner, ancestors may be encountered in their world. Note here that I deliberately omitted reports of ancestral encounters during NDEs, which have been amply described elsewhere.

Note here from the beginning that encounters in the ancestral world are reported as being almost always benevolent, at least in the long run. (Some psychotropic "trips" into the ancestral world do turn out less than positive, but these cases usually result from irresponsible practices–namely without the guiding hand of an experienced shaman.)

We meet up with ancestors in their metaphysical reality most often in our dreams, as seen in more than half of such cases. Noteworthy is that these dreams are hardly ever nightmares–although they may well be ominous–but instead are almost always solicitous visits to help us out on our destiny paths. The shamanic advice to pay close attention to our dreams and their interpretation–especially the meaning of their symbols–is well taken. If we ignore ancestral dreams, we may be missing out on valuable personal information, not to mention writing off the accumulated wisdom of our heritage.

Next, we encounter ancestral reality during deliberate SSCs, as seen in the remaining cases totaling almost one-half. Usually these meetings occur in the course of a shamanic journey of some kind, possibly after ingesting a psychotropic plant like ayahuasca or iboga, but also during shaman-guided vision quests, walkabouts, or sittings-out. So, if you want to meet up with the Old Ones in their reality, go to sleep or call a shaman.

In short, aside from the purposely excluded encounters, where are you most likely to meet your ancestors? In your world. Is this a good thing? It could go either way. If the encounter goes south, call a shaman to protect you and straighten things out. What about encounters in their world? Bet on a useful meeting, and enjoy the trip into the Land of the Deceased. It'll be a preview of coming attractions.

CHAPTER 9

In the Footsteps of the Ancestors

People will not look forward to posterity who never look backward to their ancestors.

Irish philosopher Edmund Burke

We have our Old Ones for a reason–they are, like it or not, with us for the long haul. To ignore them is to miss a major point of our being here in earth school, namely to learn lessons about our life from the afterlife. It would be like playing hooky for the whole first half of a school year and then expecting not to flunk out.

I'm talking here about destiny. Our ancestors have gone into the afterlife and we will too, and so we going to walk in their footsteps whether we accept it or not. They have a lot to show us on our way. We can ignore them or heed them. Most often today we ignore them, and then suffer the consequences.

Lessons from the Lineages

Here's a little story to illustrate. During one of my camping trips into the Bob Marshall Wilderness with a group of volunteers, one of our members, a medical doctor, accidentally cut a gash in his hand that started bleeding profusely. Since

I had been researching, teaching, and publishing about the medicinal uses of wild plants for many years, and had even earned a Certificate in Wilderness Medicine, I started right away to look for yarrow and, as expected, spotted a patch nearby. I told him, "There's some yarrow, a great styptic and an antiseptic and anti-inflammatory to boot." He looked at me as if I had just crawled out of a cave. He was panicked and befuddled without all his modern equipment and supplies. Then, for reasons I'll never fathom, he ran off to our latrine area, dripping blood all the way and back again. Then he put some superglue on the cut, which didn't help. So he packed up his gear and left us in a rush, half-running several miles back to the trailhead parking lot, from where he drove to a hospital emergency room, dripping all the way.

So here's the question: What if he had respected the ancient herbal wisdom of his ancestors? He could have stopped the bleeding and healed the wound, then enjoyed the rest of the outing. Could have.

Just to be clear, I didn't crawl out of a cave just yesterday, I'm not a neoprimitive throwback, and I do love my chainsaw, smartphone, and Honda. Just sayin' . . . let's appreciate our ancestral blessings and not, as Grandpa used to say, look a gift horse in the mouth.

Justine Baker, a Native-American Medicine Woman of the Cherokee people, put it clearly: "The . . . Earth . . . cannot be mended if we ignore the teachings of our ancestors." With global crises looming, we need all the help we can get from wherever we can get it. If the ancestors are so dumb and we are so smart, then why are we in such a mess? Maybe if we work with the ancestors to balance our world with theirs, our world won't collapse. As some African tribespeople put it, harmony between ancestors and descendants is necessary for achieving harmony in the natural world. According to Bhola Nath Banstola, "People have sought to nurture good relations with nature . . . through revering the ancestors." Or as American medium Diana Paxson put it, "Powers are reaching out to us because we are their children, and together we need to save our world." Destiny entanglement. Teamwork.

Takeaways

So here are a few practical items from the shamanic take on engaging the Old Ones that may prove to be useful to you, yours, and the rest of us.

{} Modern people have yet to realize that global crises are not good for their descendants. So, play benevolent ancestor right now in your daily life by caring about your progeny and theirs on down the line. Plan your activities like the Iroquois: Before doing anything, take into account how it will affect the next seven generations. Too, honor your ancestors by leaving a shining spiritual legacy for your–and *their*–descendants to emulate.

{} Dig into your ancestral lore. Since the beginning of knowledge is the knowledge of ignorance, admit that, while your ancestors know you well, the reverse is far from true. Investigate at least the stories about your immediate Old Ones, so you can talk intelligently with them about their lives and not just yours. Ancestral connection is a two-way street.

{} Ancestral grandparents are spiritually special, so pay attention to your living ones now. Get to know them well and they may prove uniquely helpful to you later on from their afterlives.

{} Ancestors, though, are a mixed bag. Be sure to look into the less than savory aspects of their lives. After all, their dark energy may have been, and maybe will be, visited upon you. So be careful when making out your guest list.

{} Their most likely gift is actionable information; their most likely plague is psychological distress. To maximize benefits and minimize costs, contact a shaman, preferably a psychopomp. Really. They can offer an overview of the terrain, experience, insight, protection, ceremonial expertise, and other services.

{} Connection without clinging is the aim. Clinging is for babies. Ancestors and descendants, while needing to stay spiritually connected, also need to let go of each other. Dragging heavy baggage from your lineage along your destiny path is way too much work. So, love your ancestors deeply and let them deeply love you, but establish respect for each other's freedom. Why? Because all souls need to evolve and freedom is necessary to do so, whereas clinging and being clung to promotes the opposite. Clinging keeps everyone stuck–it stops growth. Let freedom ring.

{} Control the encounters by setting clear boundaries from the start. Connect on *your* terms. For example just say, "Don't disturb my life unless something urgent needs to be done." You don't want more than you bargained for. Ghost sickness is no joke. Your mantra needs to be: *Keep a respectful distance.* That is, close enough to enjoy each other's company, but not so close as to interfere with your survival routines. Then, when you do want to connect, you can bring in all that good food and drink, flowers, song, and of course dance. Then get ready to fill that hole in your soul with ancestral grace.

{} But those boundaries will break down if your spiritual life is less than admirable. Practice energy hygiene now by enlightening and empowering yourself, making your energy body sparkling bright. Become a spiritual hero in your own mind, and help your ancestors become the same. Then you and they can evolve, in this life and the next. As a team. Having fun. Dancing.

Glossary

Ancestor-deficit disorder. A feeling of emptiness, especially among Euroamericans, deriving from historical loss of ancestral connections.

Ancestor effect. The improvement of performance on a task when ancestors are recalled.

Chi. Chinese term for the current of power that fuels and flows through a creature's energy body; aka Korean and Japanese *ki*, and other such words in various cultures.

Clan ancestors. Deceased souls who lived in the remote past over a large geographical area and who belong to an entire extended family that reaches back over many generations; also remote ancestors.

Co-evolution. The achievement of a higher level of wisdom and power by souls as a result of mutual assistance between ancestors and living descendants; the beneficial result of their entangled destinies.

Defamiliarizing effect. Repelling undesired ancestors from a scene by making it unrecognizable and uncomfortable.

Destiny entanglement. The mutuality of purpose and meaning between the souls of ancestors and their living descendants.

Effigy. A material artifact that represents or symbolizes an ancestor or an object meaningful to them.

Elemental nature-spirit. The special energy associated with a basic building block of nature, such as Earth, Water, and so on—the exact number varying with culture.

Energetic resonance. The vibrational feeling of having merged one's energy body with that of an ancestor, as a result of the two energy bodies having similar energetic signatures.

Energy body. The template that forms and moves the physical body; also energy field; also, when seen outlining the physical body, the aura.

Energy hygiene. The clearing of darknesses and blockages from one's energy body in order to strengthen and protect it from another's unwanted influence.

Energy signature. The unique configuration of one's energy body that is similar to that of one's ancestors and descendants.

Familiarizing effect. Attracting desired ancestors to a scene by making it recognizable and comfortable.

Immediate ancestors. Recently deceased souls who are usually well known to their living descendants.

Lineage curse. The inflicting of maladies on successive generations of a family line by an ancestor or other spiritual entity.

Name invocation. Speaking the appellations of ancestors aloud in order to attract their attention for the sake of making contact.

Name silence. Avoiding the speaking of the appellations of ancestors in order to prevent any contact.

Negative trigger. A physical object or action intended to displease ancestors so as to repel them from a scene.

NDE. Near-death experience; the temporary separation of the soul from the body as a result of serious physical misfortune, followed by the soul's return to the body.

Non-sanguinary "ancestors." Caregivers during one's upbringing who were outside of one's family but who acted in loco parentis, and who subsequently died and to whom one still feels emotionally connected.

Place and time locks. The determination of a specific locale and historical period that one wishes to reach during a journey from physical to metaphysical reality, in order to meet an ancestor from that locale and period; also itinerary.

Plant-spirit. The unique life force of a botanical species or higher taxonomical level.

Positive trigger. A physical object or action intended to please ancestors so as to attract them to a scene.

Power place. A site viewed as especially meaningful and powerful for a spiritual experience.

Power time. An occasion viewed as especially meaningful and powerful for a spiritual experience.

Psychopomp. A shaman or medium who guides deceased souls into a peaceful afterlife.

Remote ancestors. Deceased souls who died well before their living descendants were born and who belong to an entire clan, tribe, or culture; also clan ancestors.

Sanguinary ancestors. Deceased members of one's biological lineage.

Shaman. Person who works with spiritual entities to affect both physical and metaphysical realities.

Shamanic journey. A soul trip taking a spiritual practitioner from physical to metaphysical reality and back again.

Spirit plate. A dish of food set out in order to please an ancestor.

SSC. Shamanic state of consciousness; an altered perception enabling one to interact with spiritual entities.

Transfiguration. The morphing of a descendant's face into that of an ancestor as a result of the ancestor's temporary possession of the descendant's physical body.

Chapter Endnotes

Opening Paxson epigraph: 2015:125

Introduction

Jarvis epigraph: https://www.goodreads.com/quotes/tag/ancestors Accessed 18 July 2019

As American ghost hunter Karen Stevens put it: 2010:163

Although the word originated: Muesse, 2003:62

With this term: Charles, 1953

Yet this kind of work: but see Pratt, 2007, 2019b, 2019c

In Siberia's Buryatia: Tkacz, 2016

Since systematic and detailed knowledge: Harner, 2008-2011

In Polynesia: Sacred Hoop, 2019b: 36

As two experienced ghost hunters: Brueski & Brueski, 2017

Of course if we go back: Wilcox, 2004

According to Karen Stevens: 2010:233

A telling story: Long & Perry, 2016:74-75

As American medium: Wands, 2006:128

American researchers: Long and Perry, 2016:149-150, 154-156; see also Atwater 2003

They are sometimes revered: Katz, 1999

A common name: Eliade, 1992:40

Mayans in Central America: Pieper, 2007

In Korea: Menges, 1983

To Polynesians: Sacred Hoop, 2019b

For example some NDErs: Long, 2010:126-127

Other terms: Fischer et al., 2011:14

Such Old Ones: Stavis, 2018

Adoptees during NDEs: D. Linn et al., 2016:53

Second, those with non-sanguinary lineages: Kawabori, 2019

Ancient Egypt: Garland, 2012.

Chapter

1 Shamans and Ancestors

Tesla epigraph: www.goodreads.com/author/quoptes/278. Nikola_Tesla Accessed 4 May 2017

So, as modern practitioner: MacEowen, 2001a:9

But in the past several decades: Kowalewski, 2019a

In fact, according to a global survey: www.adherents.com Accessed 6 June 2019

They are usually the first: Kowalewski, 2015

By preserving ancestral knowledge: Filan & Kaldera, 2013

Celtic shamans: MacLeod, 2019

Yet shamans know the difference: Kowalewski, 2012

Shamans, then, as acclaimed scholar Mircea Eliade noted: 1992:12

Modern practitioner Frank MacEowen: 2001b:15, 18

The great gods of Korean shamans: Menges, 1983

Okinawan shamans: Ohashi et al., 1984:72

Among Fijians: Katz, 1999

Mexican shamans: Rasbold, 2019

Scandinavian Sami shamans: Balzer, 1987; Price, 2004

In native communities: de Angulo, 1926:355; Harner, 2006

The Huichols of Mexico: Furst, 2005

In many cultures: Kowalewski, 2014; MacEowen, 2001b:15-16; see too Hurston, 1931; Schiavi, 2018

This is hardly surprising: Martin & Romanovski, 1997:8

Such transmission may derive: Dixon, 1908; Peters, 1981

The shamans of California's Paviotso culture: Park, 1934

Some Japanese shamans: Fairchild, 1962; Noll & Shi, 2004

For many Mongolian ones: Carey, 2019; Haslund, 2019; Sodnom, 2019; Tedlock, 2005; Todd, 2010

Among the Darkhads in Mongolia: Turner, 2019; see too Tkacz, 2016

The Ulchi shamans of Siberia: van Ysslestyne, 2019b

My Polish surname: Czaplicka, 2010; Eliade, 1979;.Sacred Hoop, 2007:22; Wood, 2014

The Bambara culture of West Africa: Bailey, 2015

So too have the Tibetan: Sacred Hoop, 2007

In Mongolian and Siberian regions: Sacred Hoop, 2007:22; Wood, 2014

In Siberia's Kolyma district: Czaplicka, 2010:27

Among the Yakut: Czaplicka, 2010

In Nepal: Hitchcock, 1967; Peters, 1999; Riboli, 1994

In Finnish shamanism: Harle, 2019

In Siberian shamanism: Abgey, 2019:34

The Tamang people of Nepal: Peters, 1999

In many shamanic cultures: Cheung, 2006; Lecouteux, 2009; Louis, 1999; Sacred Hoop, 2007; Wood, 2014

For this reason in Egypt: Cheung, 2006; Rasbold, 2019

Such may happen to Wintu: Berndt, 1946; Krippner et al;, 2002; Thomas, 2018

The calling may take the form of an NDE: Kowalewski, 2014; 2015; Pearson, 2014; Sartori, 2014

Who better than someone who has visited: Sutherland, 1989

A Korean may be called: Engblom, 1992

Siberian Tungusic, Mayan, and Aboriginal shamans: Omega Institute, 2002, 2003

Shamans in Siberia: Basilov, 1989a

Khanty shamans: Balzer, 1987; Ryan, 1999

In Senegal: Martinez, 2019

Celtic ancestors: MacEowan, 1998

Mayan ancestors: Pieper, 2007

Zulu ones: Koloko, 2002

In North America: Kipp, 1996

Shamans may be called specifically: Eliade, 1992:67

Huichols: Esima, 2019; Furst, 2005; Grimaldi, 2019; Hitchcock, 1967

The call may come via a dream: Eliade, 1992

Mongolian ancestor-shamans: Odigan, 2018; Schweitzer, 2019

Future Guarani shamans: Keeney, 2003b; Riboli, 1994

Fijian shamans: Katz, 1999

As Michael Harner put it: 2006:21

The new Buryat initiate: Tkacz, 2016

Tamang shamans: Peters, 1990

In Japan: Fairchild, 1962

So also do the Hmong shamans: Mottin, 1984

In fact, the *main* spirit helper: Bellospirito, 2019; Tkacz, 2016

New shamans in Korea: Kendall, 1988:445

Hmong shamans: Lemoine, 1996

They get, as it were: Luks, 1991; Rowan et al., 1999; van der Linden, 2011

In Southwest Africa: Keeney, 2005

The Buryat shaman's knowledge: Tkacz, 2016:92.

Native-American shamans: Dixon, 1908; Park, 1934

Among the Osage: Calpine, 1996

Celtic scholarship notes: Matthews, 2012:109

Mayan shamans too: Pieper, 2007

In Nepal as well: Pratt, 2007

In North America: Moss, 2003

Ancestral parents of Zulu shamans: Koloko, 2002

An ancestor will teach Fijian shamans: Katz, 1981:69

An ancestor will also help shamans: Raven Wing, 2001

In Buryatia: Tkacz, 2002

So too do Nepalese shamans: Banstola & Rysdyk, 2019:22

Guarani shamans: Keeney, 2003b

Sami shamans: Joy, 2009

Korean shamans pay homage: Pallant, 2009

The ancestors of Mexican shamans: Rasbold, 2019

Uighur shamans in China: Beller-Hann, 2001b

According to Bhola Nath Banstola: Banstola & Rysdyk, 2019:xxi

In Mongolia: Rubin, 2019b

As this shaman welcomes: Carey, 2019

Darkhad shamans: Turner, 2019

Aborigine shamans: Berndt, 1946

The same has been found among Native-Americans: Dixon, 1908

Among the Toba in Argentina: Miller, 1975

This has also been the case for the Oroqen: Noll & Shi, 2004

Siberian Tuvan shamans: Pfeiffer, 2003

Mayan shamans: Tedlock, 2006

Siberian Chukchi shamans: Basilov, 1989a:20; Wahbeh, 2019

Celtic shamans of old: Matthews, 2012

Western shamans today: Kowalewski, 2015; Moss, 2006

One uses her ancestors: Stavis, 2018

Energetic signature: Kowalewski, 2019b

In Japan: Miyake, 2001

Such transmission across generations: Noll & Shi, 2004:11

One in ten people: Martin & Romanowski, 1997

If there's a way to communicate: Guggenheim & Guggenheim, 1995; Holland, 2018; D. Linn et al., 2016; Wright, 1999

A practitioner can ask them: Balzer, 1996

Traditional Africans: Drosin, 1995

The ancestors of clients of a Bushmen shaman: Keeney, 2003a

Shamans elsewhere: Moss, 2006

As Chumpi, a Shuar shaman of the Amazon: Perkins, 2001:20

Likewise in West Africa: Blair, 2008

According to one Euroamerican participant: Blair, 2008:50

In Vodou as well: Heaven, 2003

A Japanese family may invite: Fairchild, 1962

One modern shaman-exorcist: Stavis, 2018

For example, in one difficult case: Kowalewski, 2015

As such the journey feels: Matthews, 2018:32

2   Getting No Respect

Maalouf epigraph: https://www.goodreads.com/quotes/tag/ancestors Accessed 13 March 2019

As Peruvian Q'ero leader Benito Apaza: Sims, 2019:73

But when the churches came along: Lecouteux 2009

Some churches even forbade: Harris, 1919

In the Middle Ages: Martin & Romanowski, 1997

Islamic clerics: Lorimer, 1929; Sidky, 1994; Staley, 1982; Wood, 2006, 2019b

Voltaire: https://brainyquote.com/topics/ancestors Accessed 13 June 2019

In short, the Enlightenment: Anagnost, 1987:43

The breaking apart of families: Thornton, 1988:276

Repression of spiritual ceremonies: Hurston, 1931

The American South availed itself: Rasbold, 2019:38, 67

According to an ancestor-shaman: Ferrer, 2019:57

Traditional African cultures: Bailey, 2015

But if we do that: Drosin, 1995

The ancient Celts: Wright, 1997; MacEowen, 1998

We also find a Norse tradition: Kaldera & Krasskova, 2012

Too, the Q'ero people: Sacred Hoop, 2019a

Americans are also asserting: Fournier, 2018:66

An online summit of spiritual practitioners: Kowalewski, 2019

The tradition of ancestral honoring: Wood, 2019b

3   Why Ancestors Matter

Beller-Hann epigraph: 2001a:11

Several studies have documented: Fischer et al., 2011; https://digest.bpi.org.uk/2010/12/20/the-benefits -of thinking-about-our-ancestors Accessed 15 May 2019

In Vodou: Heaven, 2003

In Japanese shamanism: Miyake, 2001

Mediums report: Van Praagh, 2009

According to Aborigines: Bell, 1999

A number of traditions: Ryan, 1999

In many cultures: Filan & Kaldera, 2013:2

The ancestors, say some Native-Americans: Moses, 1998:44

Mohawks, for example, claim: Moss, 2006:25

According to Western shaman Robert Moss: 2006:25

In Celtic tradition: Matthews, 2012, 2018:35

Likewise in Polynesia: Sacred Hoop, 2019b

Western practitioners might add: Kowalewski, 2000

We came from the metaphysical realm: Some, 1997

In fact our destiny's connection: Dyer & Garnes, 2015; Hallett, 1995; Hinze, 1997; Lundahl & Widdison, 1995; Nightingale, 2016; Tallmadge & Simons, 2015

Some mothers: Atwater, 2003:136.

In short, growing evidence: Atwater, 2003

As American root doctor Orion Foxwood put it: 2012:184

Another American practitioner: Stavis, 2018

American Granny Magicians: Rasbold, 2019

Still another points to the concern: Wands, 2006:19-20, 35-37

Vietnamese-American elders say the same thing: Wright, 2006

Our destinies, then, are wrapped up: Kowalewski, 2016

Africans, in fact, say: Bailey, 2015

Ancestors, in short: Moss, 2006

As African-American playwright: Cited in AARP The Magazine, 2019:59

In contrast, as the Zulu tradition: Lockley, 2017:xviv

To the Celts: Matthews, 2012

The Xhosa people of South Africa: Lockley, 2019:16

The West African Dagara people: Martin, 2008:7

In Norse tradition: Kaldera & Krasskova, 2012

The Q'ero people honor power spots: Williams, 2007

A Mexican shaman: Rasbold, 2019

Buryat shaman: Tkacz, 2016:90, 96

In Guatemala, Quiche shamans: Makransky, 2019

Fijians too say: Katz, 1999

The ancestors, that is: D. Linn et al., 2016:54, 154

Psychics report: Bodine, 2013

Often these guides: Matthews, 2019; Wands, 2006

For good reason, then: https://www.goodreads.com/quotes/tag/ancestors Accessed 23 May 2019

An ancestor can point you: Caputo, 2013

Hospital patients with mysterious maladies: D. Linn et al., 2016

Native-American ancestors: Cheung, 2006

In the American Ozark and Appalachian mountains: Rasbold, 2019

Quiche practitioners: Makransky, 2019

Gypsy shamans: Lee, 1999

Buryat shamans: Shaman's Drum, 2000

Among the Ulchi: Louis, 1999

Tanzanian Sukuma shamans: Winkelman & Peek, 2004

Vodou ones sing songs: Heaven, 2018

Mongolian ones may merge: Rubin, 2019

Korean ones summon: Choi, 2019

Ancestral shaman-healers: Bender, 2001; Moss, 1994

Amazonian shamans: Luna, 2006

Siberian ones too: White, 2005

In Vodou, for example: Heaven, 2018

Many writers: Martinez, 2019

Bwiti practitioners in West Africa,: Caravelli, 2008; White, 2006

To Irish shaman: Matthews, 2018:32

A modern West African shaman: Some, 1997

We can receive this wisdom: Martinez, 2019

Fijians for instance, say: Katz, 1999:318

As American writer Suzy Kassem put it: https://www.goodreads.com/quotes/tag/ancestors Accessed 3 June 2019

The ancestors are also touted: Moss, 2006

This is a very good thing: Fischer et al., 2011; Jonas et al., 2002

As American medium Jeffrey Wands put it: 2006:17

So after that shamanic journey: Kowalewski, 2002a, 2002b, 2008, 2009; Kowalewski et al., 2007

In Africa, for example: Bailey, 2015

Southern Africans say: Esima, 2019

Vietnamese-American elders: Wright, 2006

In Mongolia the ancestors of a family: Odigan, 2018

Hawaiian ancestors: Kane, 2014

In Russian folklore: Cheung, 2006

For the Buryats: Stern, 2012:131; see too Tkacz, 2016

Modern mediums too report: Mathews, 2019

Ancestors are even reported: Budapest, 2011

Many contemporary accounts: Martin & Romanowski, 1997

A colorful tale of the Hmong: Lemoine, 1996

As one anonymous experiencer put it: Long & Perry, 2016:74-75

Another NDEr: Atwater, 2003:106

Shamans often honor: Tedlock, 2005

Buryat shamans: Basilov, 1989b

The African Ibo shaman: Heaven 2003

In the Norse tradition: Kaldera & Krasskova, 2012

Same for the Fijians, Koreans, and Nepalese: Banstola & Rysdyk, 2019; Katz, 1999; Menges, 1983

Guarani shamans: Keeney, 2003b

Quiche shamans: Makransky, 2019

Bhutan shamans: Winter & Rai, 2000

The Hawaiian and other traditions: Kane, 2014

This is unsurprising: Martin & Romanowski, 1997

A favorite way the Old Ones: Caputo, 2013; Cheung, 2006; Moss, 2006; Wands, 2006

One woman, for example: Wands, 2006:57-58

For example, in Fiji: Katz, 1999

As scholarly research has pointed out: David-Barrett & Carney, 2016

Guarani shaman Ava Tape Miri put it this way: Keeney, 2003b:21

Many other kinds of help: Tein, 1994

In the Hawaiian tradition: Kane, 2014

Mongolians report: Odigan, 2018

Ancestors are also said to help: Moss, 2006

Native-American ancestors: Cheung, 2006

The Old Ones are also said: Kane, 2014

The afterlife then: Benton, 2019

According to American medium Theresa Caputo: 2013:100; see also 158

According to spiritual writer Susan Martinez: 2019

American medium Patrick Mathews: 2019:54; see too 248

The ancestors, in short, are evolving: Bodine, 2013
In Japanese shamanism: Miyake, 2001
The ancient Greeks: Garland, 2012
In African shamanism: Filan, 2007
Southern African shamans: Esima, 2019
To a Vodou practitioner: Filan, 2007
Ancestral possession of participants: Paper, 1996:120
And as medium Theresa Caputo put it: 2013:100

4 Connecting in the Physical Realm

Gonzalez epigraph: https://www.brainyquote.com/topics/ancestors Accessed 12 May 2019
As Jeffrey Wands put it: 2006:3
But shamans, like Western practitioner: Pratt, 2018
American researcher Virlana Tkacz: 2016:93.
Many shamanic traditions: Reese & Boag, 2008
Malay tribespeople: Sheat, 1902:134-135
In the Japanese tradition of shugendo: Miyake, 1989
The most common way: Fairchild, 1962; Vaudoise, 2019
These items not only reconnect us: Cole & Robson, 2015:130
Ancient Romans: Garland, 2012
In West Africa: Cheung, 2006
Vodou practitioners: Deren, 1983; www.britannica.com/topic/govi-vodou Accessed 18 June 2019
Hoodoo practitioners: Hurston, 1931
The Huichols: Allione, 1995); Furst, 2005
At the shrines of Mongolian shamans: Carey, 2019
Ancient Romans: Harl, 2011; www.italysbestrome.com/roses-and-ancient-roman-rituals/ Accessed 10 September 2018
In India: Mayatitinanda, 2005
And don't be surprised: Martin & Romanowski, 1997
Shamans will add: Kowalewski, 2007

In Ulchi culture: van Ysslestyne, 2019b:17

Korean shamans: Engblom, 1992

Buryat shamans: Balogh, 2007:111; see also Moss, 1998

As one of their chants goes: Tkacz, 2016:42

Cooked food: Beller-Hann, 2001a

And don't forget: Kowalewski, 2007

The ancient Greeks: Garland, 2012

Early Europeans: Musi, 1997

Likewise Malay tribespeople: Sheat, 1902:134-135

In fact in many parts of the world: Cheung, 2006

Some indigenes in Papua New Guinea also make: www.
blog.nms.ac.uk/2017/02/17/cemmuning-with-papuan-
ancestor-boards/ Accessed 20 August 2019

In many indigenous cultures: Furst, 1965

In West Africa: Cook, 1989; Paicheler, 2008

In the Hawaiian tradition: Kane, 2014

Yokuts in California: Gayton, 1948

Mayans make: Pieper, 2007

Ulchi and Udeghe shamans: van Ysslestyne, 2019b; Wood,
2019c

Khanty shamans: Balzer, 1987

Some indigenes in Papua New Guinea decorate: https://
www.pinterest.com/pin/391391023837581549

The kachinas also carry messages: Cheung, 2006; Voth, 2015

The Ulchi construct: van Ysslestyne, 2019b

Some indigenes in Papua New Guinea also make https://
www.pinterest.com/pin/391391023837581549 Accessed 18
July 2019

The Ulchi, for example, sing: van Ysslestyne, 2019b:17

Ulchi shamans, for example, may ask: van Ysslestyne,
2019b

The Japanese, for example: Miyake, 2001

For shamans, words are important: Tkacz, 2016:164-165

Researchers in fact have shown: Gimbel, 2015

Mohawk shamans: Moss, 2003

These inherited responses: Wolynn 2017, 2019

If you can't go physically: Dane, 2019

Tobacco and alcohol work: Kowalewski, 2007

Modern pilgrims on such treks: AARP The Magazine, 2019

Polynesians leave such gifts: Kowalewski, 2016:92-93; Sacred Hoop, 2019b

Fijians say: Katz, 1999

During the Japanese Bon festival: Miyake, 2001

Ancient Europeans: Devereux, 2008

The Celts, for example: Matthews, 2012

In Japan, for example: Fairchild, 1962

Peoples around the world: Ingerman, 2018; Some, 2017

Such has been the case: Degarrod, 1998; Engblom, 1992; Pfeiffer, 2003; White, 2005

Chinese shamans: Paper, 1996

A Hoodoo practitioner: Rasbold, 2019

Some biologists speak: Sheldrake, 2018:210, 212

Dukhan shamans: Grimaldi, 2019

Many humans joining together: Foster et al., 1996, 1998

The Yupiit people of Alaska: Fienup-Riordan, 1996

Ancient Romans made offerings: Lecouteux, 2009

A Norse tradition uses runes: Kaldera & Krasskova, 2012

Huichols, for their part: Furst, 2005

The ancient Khmers of Cambodia: Bender, 2001

Ulchi shamans make use: van Ysslestyne, 2019a

In ancient Rome: Lecouteux, 2009; see too Mathews, 2019

Say the Yaminahua shamans of Peru: Townsley, 1993:457

Not only is song: Grauds, 2001:31; Host, 2018:18-19

Since it bypasses the logical mind: Matthews, 2018:34

Ulchi shamans use song: van Ysslestyne, 2019b

At ayahuasca ceremonies: Ferrer, 2019

Ancient Celtic Druids: McLeod, 2019

Some Ika and Kogi people of Colombia: Davis, 2009

In medieval Rome: Lecouteux, 2009

Zimbabwean shamans: Van Deusen, 2005

Siberian shamans: Van Deusen, 1997-1998

Some Tuvan shamans: Amacker, 2002

The Nepalese ceremonialize: Hitchcock, 1967

According to Celtic shaman Frank MacEowen: 1998:39

The songs used by a new Oroqen shaman: Noll & Shi, 2004

Among Native-Americans: Dixon, 1908

Nepalese shamans say: Riboli, 1994

Sometimes an ancestor: Heaven, 2003

Guarani shamans are given: Keeney, 2003b

Native-Americans in the Northwest: Smith & Ryan, 1999

Bushmen shamans: Riccio, 1996

According to African Zulu shaman Patience Koloko: 2002

One Euroamerican shaman: Raven-Wing, 1997

Ulchi shamans use dance: van Ysslestyne, 2019b

Vodou shamans in New Orleans: Rasbold, 2019

Yokuts dance: Gayton, 1948

Any talk of ancestral dance: Parker, 2010

For greater power: Kowalewski, 2016

As the chant of Buryat shamans goes: Tkacz, 2016:179

In fact as often happens today: Kowalewski, 2016; Lopez et al., 2018

The Ulchi, for example: van Ysslestyne, 2019b

Buryat shamans: Balogh, 2007; Tkacz, 2016

Fijians hold a ceremony: Katz, 1999

According to Trinidadian author Wayne Trotman: https://www.goodreads.com/quotes/tag/ancestors Accessed 7 July 2019

The Quiche, for example: Makransky, 2019

Korean and Japanese shamans: Menges, 1983; Miyake, 2001

Fijians thank the ancestors: Katz, 1999

Vodou practitioners: Filan, 2007; Heaven, 2003

They should be in a good-enough mood: Robinson, 1998

Vodou practitioners: Heaven, 2003

Scientists used to tell us: D. Linn et al., 2016

Too, many NDErs go through: Caputo, 2013; Ring, 2006

In fact, mediums report: Bodine, 2013; Caputo, 2013; Wands, 2006

Other ancestors: Martin & Romanowski, 1997; Smith, 2018

This shows, as American mediums: Martin & Romanowski, 1997:176; see too Mathews, 2019:250

All three too, by clearing out unresolved issues: Martin & Romanowski, 1997

Also, by shedding the burdens: Kowalewski, 2016

With respect to forgiveness: Holland, 218;61

According to Jeffrey Wands: 2006:60

5   Connecting in the Metaphysical Realm

Hardy epigraph: https://www.brainyquote.com/topics/ancestors Accessed 13 June 2019

The Makuna people of the Amazon: Arhem, 1996

You can make a spirit visit: Harner, 2008-2011; Matthews, 2012

Mapuche shamans: de la Paz, 2005

While on such a journey: Simonsen, 2019

Some historians: Vandiver, 2014

On the other hand, Bwiti cultists: Paicheler, 2008

Indeed, more and more are saying: Kowalewski, 2015, 2016

Some try to copy: Robinson, 1998

Years later I found out: Grimaldi, 2019

Ancestral traditions: Esima, 2019

Some reports say: Degarrod, 1998

Fijians say: Katz, 1999

For the Matsigenka in Peru: Baer & Snell, 1974:73

The ethnographic literature: see Kowalewski, 2007

According to ayahuascero Fernando Payaguaje: Cabodevilla, 2003:55

Maybe this is why: Mabit, 2006:28; Metzner, 2008:43; Schinzinger, 2008:24

Likewise, Fang tribalists: Metzner, 1999; White, 2006

Fijian shamans: Katz, 1999:192

Koryak elders of Siberia: Fienup-Riordan, 1996

We may also meet up: Kowalewski, 2000, 2016

Some Euroamericans too: Endredy, 2019

In a Japanese version: Miyake, 2001

Aborigines have a like tradition: Devery, 2019; Sacred Hoop, 2013

During their trek: Grof, 2006; LaFleur, 2015

Likewise the Norse: Kaldera & Krasskova, 2012

A Scandanavian Sami: Simonsen, 2019

The Q'ero people too: Williams, 2007

Huichols also find: Ryan, 1999; Stone, 2019

Like the Aborigines: Furst, 2005:36-37

Classically the shaman: Kowalewski, 2015; Winders, 1994

6 Typical Manifestations

Harner epigraph: 2006:21

As one of my shamanic teachers: Brown, Jr.: 2007; see also Brown, Jr., 1993

American psychic Margaret Wendt: Martin and Romanowski, 1997.

Excellent books: Guggenheim & Guggenheim, 1995; Martin & Romanowski, 1997

TV series: *Long Island Medium*; *Ghost Whisperer*

The first form is found worldwide: Martin & Romanowski, 1997

In Polynesia, for example: Sacred Hoop, 2019b

The contacts may come: Martin & Romanowski, 1997

Many patients then report: Martin & Romanowski, 1997

As the descendant is passing away: Bodine, 2013:49-50

I could psychically see: Bodine, 2013:14-15; see too Martin & Romanowski, 1997; Mathews, 2019

As one previously skeptical descendant: Martin & Romanowski, 1997:171

Among the Yakut in Siberia: Balzer. 2002

In Japan, for example: Fairchild, 1962

The participants may even communicate: Miyake, 2001

Tuvan ancestors: Pfeiffer, 2003

Zapotec ones: Gordon, 2000

Dukhan shamans: Grimaldi, 2019

Aborigines, too, often see: Bell, 1999

During the Mandan Sun Dance: Irwin, 1997

The literature on mediums: Caputo, 2016; Holland, 2018; Van Praagh, 2009

The Makuna, for example: Arhem, 1996

Other peoples: Kane, 2014; Pollock, 2008; Odigan, 1999

In Polynesia, the Old Ones: Sacred Hoop, 2019b

This type of possession is not difficult: Kowalewski, 2019b

I later found out: Roland, 2102:63; Tkacz, 2016:90

According to the report of one client: Martin & Romanowski, 1997:170

Professional dream researchers: Krippner et al., 2002; Moss, 1994, 2003, 2006

But this is hardly news: Bell, 1999

Zulu descendants: Lockley, 2019

If you're unsure a dream: Adapted and expanded from Harner, 2010a, 2010b.

The Iroquois regard such dream: Moss, 1994

Later the information is verified: Martin & Romanowski, 1997

These dreams happen: Moss, 2003

7   **All Wine and Roses?**

Howe epigraph: https://www.brainyquote.com/topics/ancestors Accessed 7 June 2019

Fijians, for example: Katz, 1999

Chepang shamans in Nepal: Riboli, 2002

Some mediums, for example: Caputo, 2013; Stavis, 2018

The researchers found: Fischer et al., 2011

Indigenous cultures: Beller-Hann, 2001a; Kendall, 1988; Martinez, 2019; Paxson, 2015; Pratt 2007; Winders, 1994

The Ulchi put it bluntly: van Ysslestyne, 2019b:9

People who die with serious unresolved issues: Gayton, 1948; Kowalewski, 2015; Pratt, 2018

Buryat culture: Tkacz, 2016

They may come into our world: Moss, 2006

For this reason in ancient Greece: Cheung, 2006

The ancient Romans too: Lecouteux, 2009

Koreans today express: Kim, 1989:257

In many African cultures: Bailey, 2015

Hoodoo practitioners: Hurston, 1931

In Fiji, a story asserts: Katz, 1999

In Russian folklore: Cheung, 2006

In Melanesia, a hooligan ancestral ghost: Martinez, 2019

Ancestors who were overprotective parents: Fiore, 1987

A "familist" or "clannist" ancestor: Martinez, 2019

Other ancestors may possess: Martinez, 2019

In such cases the Khanty: Balzer, 1987; see also Kowalewski, 2015

The Inuit too report: Tein, 1994

The Washo people of California: Handelman, 1967

In Fiji too: Katz, 1999

American genealogist: Laurence Overmire, https://www.goodreads.com/quotes/tag/ancestors Accessed 29 July 2019

Ancestors may come: Panthera, 2009

Central Asian shamans: Wood, 2019b

In parts of ancient Europe: Garland, 2012

The Ewe-speaking people of West Africa: Hurston, 1931

As Suquamish Chief Seattle put it: https://www.
brainyquote.com/topics/ancestors, Accessed 20 July 2019

In ancient Germany: Lecouteux, 2009

In parts of England it is said: Cheung, 2006

The Khanty warn: Balzer 1987:1091

In Fiji an ancestor: Katz, 1999

In Korea neglected ancestors: Kendall, 1988; Kim, 1989

In Okinawa, ancestors may be upset: Ohashi et al., 1984

To Polynesians the ancestors: Sacred Hoop, 2019b:37

In Japan, ancestors who are not honored: Miyake, 2001

Okinawan shamans often attribute: Ohashi et al. 1984

In the Hawaiian tradition: Kane, 2014

In India, angry ancestors: Dwyer, 1998

During the Mexican Day of the Dead: Cheung, 2006

Ancestors who are stuck: Kowalewski, 2015

Hoodoo practitioners: Rasbold, 2019

Such ancestors who just benefit themselves: Martinez, 2019:239

Note here that both: Villoldo, 1996

Such fields have been well known: Omega Institute, 2002, 2003

According to ethnographic studies: Alvino, 1996

But as American researcher: Bache, 2009:92

This means that energy bodies: Guggenheim & Guggenheim, 1995; Oschman, 2003, 2015; Proud, 2015

Some reports tell: Martinez, 2019; Maurey, 1988

Among the Nage of Indonesia: Forth, 1991

Hoodoo practitioners say: Hurston, 1931

In Mexico a common shamanic practice: Alarcon, 2001; Rasbold, 2019; Williams, 1999

Ancient Greeks likewise: Garland, 2012

Some Native-Americans too believe: Cheung, 2006

In Korea, a survivor: Engblom, 1992; Kendall, 1988

Modern psychic: Wands, 2006:71

British medium: Smith, 2018:6

A Cuban Santeria shaman: Brown, 2005

A Zapotec story: Gordon, 2000:19

For Polynesians too: Sacred Hoop, 2019b:37

Among Native-American Salish people: Haebertin, 2019

The Bushmen too say: Katz et al., 1997

In a report about the Bushmen: Riccio, 1996

In fact the attribution: Krippner, 2008; James Lawless, www.vision-voyages.com/ancestral-healing.html Accessed 13 June 2019 ; Winders, 1994

In Fiji, for example: Katz, 1999

In the Himalayas: Winders, 1994

In turn, the curses may cause: Pratt, 2019a

That is, spiritual pathologies: Silvana, 2009

Some shamans, then, speak: Silvana, 2009:4

This is a spiritual sickness: Miro-Quesada, 2019

Still other practitioners speak: Stavis, 2018:181

We can even find: Isaacson, 2009a, 2009b; Scott and Isaacson, 2009; see also Martinez, 2019

An outside curse of a lineage: Stavis, 2018:78-21

As American shaman: Gunshore, 2019:48

Over the millennia: Foor, 2017

For example, they know: Tedlock, 2005

Mapuche shamans: Bacigalupo, 1998

Some Native-Americans: Wood, 2019a

The Korean shaman: Engblom, 1992; Kim, 1989

In some parts of the U.S. South: Hurston, 1931; Rasbold, 2019

In Mongolia, for example: Odigan, 1999
Native-Americans are known: Cheung, 2006
An Inuit community may refrain: Tein, 1994
The Yokuts may even take: Gayton, 1948
As paranormal investigator Karen Stevens put it: 2007:245
The Kulina people of Brazil: Pollock, 2008
In some cultures: Cheung, 2006
In New Zealand, the Maori stomp: Sacred Hoop, 2019b
Some Native-Americans: Cheung, 2006
Others burn it: Gayton, 1948
Mexican shamans too will smudge: Rasbold, 2019
An Inuit shaman: Tein, 1994
Ancient Romans: Garland, 2012
One modern medium advises: Wands, 2006
Getting rid of the deceased's possessions: Cheung, 2006
Polynesians, for example: Sacred Hoop, 2019b:37
Gypsies too will burn: Lee, 1999
Among the Lakota: Little Eagle, 2000
The Salish too: Haebertin, 2019
Yokuts bury: Gayton, 1948:46
Ancient Europeans: Sacred Hoop, 2007
Some Inuit, for example: Tein, 1994
They confront directly: Beller-Hann, 2001a:12
When Korean shamans: Engblom, 1992; Kim, 1989
Mexican-American shamans: Rasbold, 2019
A Tuvan shaman may call out: Amacker, 2002
In Egypt a ceremony: Marinez, 2019
Some modern shamans journey: See Pratt, 2019a
When mischief occurs: Bear, 2019
A Santeria shaman may be summoned: Brown, 2005
Salish shamans, for example: Haebertin, 2019
To the Ulchi, for example: van Ysslestyne, 2019b:9
During certain ceremonies in ancient Rome: Lecouteux, 2009

Likewise, during a special Japanese festival: Miyake, 2001

A Bushmen shaman, for example: Katz et al., 1997

8 Outcome Data

Ritter epigraph: https://www.goodreads.com/quotes/tag/ancestors Accessed 29 June 2019

I made a rough: Gurr, 1972

In the words of American filmmaker Raquel Cepeda: https://www.goodreads.com/quotes/tag/ancestors Accessed 7 May 2019

Note here that I deliberately omitted: Ring, 2006

9 In the Footsteps of the Ancestors

Burke epigraph: https://www.brainyquote.com/topics/ancestors Accessed 23 April 2019

Since I had been researching: Kowalewski, 2002a, 2007

Justine Baker: 2019:48

As some African tribespeople put it: Lockley, 2019

According to Bhola Nath Banstola: Banstola & Rysdyk, 2019:xxi

Or as American medium Diana Paxson put it: 2015:255

References

AARP The Magazine. 2019. "A Return to Your Roots." October-November:56-61.

Abgey, Heidi. 2019. "The Tale of the Toli." Sacred Hoop 102a:34-35.

Alarcon, Rocio. 2001. "Plant Healing in Ecuador." International Herbal Conference, Wheaton College, Norton, MA, July.

Allione, Costanzo. 1995. Where the Eagles Fly. New York, NY: Mystic Fire Video.

Alvino, G. 1996. "The Human Energy Field in Relation to Science, Consciousness, and Health." Retrieved from www.stealthskater.com/documents/consciousness_22.doc Accessed 22 November.

Amacker, Robert. 2002. "An American in Tuva: The Education of a Reluctant Shaman." Shaman's Drum 61 (Spring):46-58.

Anagnost, Ann. 1987. "Politics and Magic in Contemporary China." Modern China 13, 1 (January):40-61.

Arhem, Kaj. 1996. Makuna: Portrait of an Amazonian People. Washington, D.C.: Smithsonian Institution.

Atwater, P.M.H. 2003. New Children and Near-Death Experiences. Rochester, VT: Bear.

Bache, Christopher. 2009. "Living classroom." Pp. 82-93 in E. Laszlo (ed.), Akashic Experience: Science and the Cosmic Memory Field. Rochester, VT: Inner Traditions.

Bacigalupo, Ana. 1998. "The Exorcising Sounds of Warfare: The Performance of Shamanic Healing and the Struggle to Remain Mapuche." Anthropology of Consciousness 9, 2-3:1-16.

Baer, G., & W. Snell. 1974. "Ayahuasca Ceremony among the Matsigenka." Zeitschrift fur Ethnologie 99, 1-2:63-80.

Bailey, Julius. 2015. Great Mythologies of the World. Chantilly, VA: Teaching Company.

Baker, Justine. 2019. "Gift of the Mask." Sacred Hoop 102:48-51.

Balogh, M. 2007. "Shamanic Traditions, Rites, and Songs among the Mongolian Buriads." Shaman 15, 1-2:87-116.

Balzer, Marjorie. 1987. "Behind Shamanism: Siberian Khanty Cosmology and Politics." Social Science Medicine 24, 12:1085-1093.

_____. 1996. "Flights of the Sacred: Symbolism and Theory in Siberian Shamanism." American Anthropologist 98, 2 (June):305-318.

_____. 2002. "Healing Failed Faith: Contemporary Siberian Shamans." Anthropology and Humanism 26, 2:128-149.

Banstola, Bhola Nath, & Evelyn Rysdyk. 2019. The Nepalese Shamanic Path. Rochester, VT: Destiny.

Basilov, 1989a. "Chosen by the Spirits." Soviet Anthropology and Archeology (Summer):9-37.

_____, 1989b. "Twilight of Shamanism." Soviet Anthropology and Archeology (Summer):38-55.

Bear, Jaya. 2019. "In the Morning of the World." Sacred Hoop 102c:40-46.

Bell, Hannah. 1999. "Songs of Creation, Songs of Death: Growing Wise in Ngarinyin Culture." Shaman's Drum 53 (Fall):28-34.

Beller-Hann, Ildiko. 2001a. "'Making the Oil Fragrant': Dealings with the Supernatural among the Uighurs in Xinjiang." Asian Ethnicity 2, 1 (March):9-23.

_____. 2001b. "Rivalry and Solidarity among Uighur Healers in Uzbekistan." Inner Asia 3, 1:71-96.

Bellospirito, Robyn. 2019. "Arshaan: Holy Water from the Spirits." Sacred Hoop 102:41-43.

Bender, Tom. 2001. "Portals to the Spirit World: Connecting with the Chi of Creation." Shaman's Drum 59 (Summer):32-45.

Benton, Gemma. 2019. "Reweaving Your Ancestral Story." https://theshiftnetwork.com/yourancestralstory Accessed 27 April.

Berndt, R. 1946. "Wuradjeri Magic and Clever Men." Oceania 17, 4:327-368.

Blair, Kristine. 2008. "Blindfolded in Order to See: Encounters with the Spirit of Iboga." Shaman's Drum 76:42-50.

Bodine, Echo. 2013. What Happens When We Die? Novato, CA: New World Library.

Brown, Catherine. 2005. "Blessed by a Santero's Flowers and Herbs." Shaman's Drum 69:55-58.

Brown, Tom, Jr. 1993. Awakening Spirits: A Native-American Path to Inner Peace, Healing, and Spiritual Growth. New York, NY: Berkley.

_____. 2007. "Way of the Shaman." Workshop, Tracker School, St. Petersburg, FL, December.

Brueski, Tony, & Jenny Brueski. 2017. Real Ghost Stories. Berkeley, CA: Ulysses.

Budapest, Z. 2011. Grandmother Moon. New York, NY: Create Space.

Cabodevilla, M. "The Old Yage Drinker's Visions." Shaman's Drum 65:52-60.

Calpine, Louie. 1996. "Early Training of an Osage Medicine Man." Shaman's Drum 42 (Summer):55-57.

Caputo, Theresa. 2013. There's More to Life than This. New York, NY: Atria.

Carey, Sas. 2019. "Reindeer Herders in My Heart." Sacred Hoop 102a:6-14.

Chamovitz, Daniel. 2012. What a Plant Knows. New York, NY: Scientific American.

Charles, Lucile. 1953. "Drama in Shaman Exorcism." Journal of American Folklore 66, 260 (April-June):95-122.

Cheung, Theresa. 2006. Element Encyclopedia of Ghosts and Hauntings. London, U.K.: HarperElement.

Choi, Daniel. 2019. "Field Notes from a Kut." Shaman's Drum 102:24-29.

Cole, Jeff, & Jonathon Robson. 2015. Ghostly Encounters: Confessions of a Paranormal Investigator. New York, NY: Skyhorse.

Cook, Pat. 1989. "Kuna Indian Song Healers of the San Blas Islands." Shaman's Drum 40 (Summer):41-45.

Czaplicka, Maria. 2010. "Coat of Power." Sacred Hoop 68:26-29.

Dane, Heather. 2019. "Are You a Generational Pattern Shifter?" Ancestral Healing Summit, Shift Network, www.theshiftnetwork.com Accessed 21 April.

David-Barrett, T., & J. Carney. 2016. "The Depiction of Historical Figures and the Emergence of Prehistoric Ancestor Veneration as a Solution to a Network Coordination Problem." Religion, Brain, and Behavior 6 (4):307-317.

Davis, Wade. 2009. "On Preserving the Diversity of the Ethnosphere." Shaman's Drum 80:30-45.

de Angulo, Jaime. 1926. "The Background of the Religious Feeling in a Primitive Tribe." American Anthropologist 28:352-360.

Degarrod, Lydia, 1998. "Female Shamanism and the Mapuche Transformation into Christian Chilean Farmers." Religion 28:339-350.

de la Paz, Mariela. 2005. "Journeys into the Realm of the Ancestors." Shaman's Drum 69:73.

Deren, Maya. 1983. Divine Horsemen: The Living Gods of Haiti. New York, NY: McPherson.

Devereux, Paul. 2008. The Long Trip: A Prehistory of Psychodelia. New York, NY: Penguin.

Devery, Darlene. 2019. "Dreamtime Visions." Sacred Hoop 102b:117-119.

Dixon, Roland. 1908. "Some Aspects of the American Shaman." Journal of American Folklore 21, 80 (January-March):1-12.

Drosin, Jay. 1995. "Papa Nlandu's Rites of Protection." Shaman's Drum 39 (Fall):49-53.

Dwyer, Graham. 1998. "The Phenomenology of Supernatural Malaise." Social Analysis 42, 2 (July):3-23.

Dyer, Wayne, & Dee Garnes. 2015. Memories of Heaven: Children's Astounding Recollections of the Time before They Came to Earth. Carlsbad, CA: Hay House.

Eliade, Mircea. 1979. The Forge and the Crucible. Chicago, IL: Chicago University Press.

_____. 1992. Shamanism: Archaic Techniques of Ecstasy. Princeton, NJ: Princeton University Press.

Engblom, John. 1992. "Bridge to Heaven: The Korean Mudang as Psychopomp." Shaman's Drum 26 (Winter): 46-54.

Endredy, James. 2019. Shamanic Alchemy. Rochester, VT: Bear.

Esima, Gogo Ekhaya. 2019. "Initiations into Ancestral Wisdom." Ancestral Healing Summit, Shift Network, www.theshiftnetwork.com Accessed 21 April.

Fairchild, William. 1962. "Shamanism in Japan." Folklore Studies 21:1-122.

Ferrer, Jorge. 2019. "Faith in Ayahuasca: An Interview with Guillermo Arevelo." Sacred Hoop 102b:56-61.

Fienup-Riordan, Ann. 1996. "Agayuliyararput: The Yup'ik Way of Making Prayers." Shaman's Drum 42 (Summer):32-41.

Filan, Kenaz. 2007. The Haitian Vodou Handbook. Rochester, VT: Destiny.

_____, & Raven Kaldera. 2013. Talking to the Spirits. Rochester, VT: Inner Traditions.

Fiore, Edith. 1987. Unquiet Dead. New York, NY: Delphi.

Fischer, P., A. Sauer, C. Vogrincic, & S. Weisweiler. 2011. "The Ancestor Effect: Thinking about Our Genetic Origin Enhances Intellectual Performance." European Journal of Social Psychology 41:11-16.

Foor, Daniel. 2017. Ancestral Medicine. Rochester, VT: Bear.

Forth, Gregory. 1991. "Shamanic Powers and Mystical Practices among the Nage of Central Flores." Canberra Anthropology 14, 2:1-29.

Foster, R., G, Bradish, Y. Dobyns, B. Dunne, & R. Jahn. 1996. "Field REG Anomalies in Group Situations." Journal of Scientific Exploration 10, 1:111-141.

_____. 1998. "Field REG II–Consciousness Field Effects: Replications and Explorations." Journal of Scientific Exploration 12, 3:425-454.

Fournier, Elizabeth. 2018. "Lay Your Loved Ones to Rest: Performing a Home Funeral." Self-Reliance (Winter):66-69.

Foxwood, Orion. 2012. The Candle and the Crossroads. San Francisco, CA: Weiser.

Furst, Peter. 1965. "West Mexican Tomb Structures as Evidence for Shamanism in Prehispanic Mesoamerica." Antropologica 15:29-80.

———. 2005. "The Visionary Art of Jose Benitez Sanchez." Shaman's Drum 69:32-41.

Garland, Robert. 2012. The Other Side of History: Daily Life in the Ancient World. Chantilly, VA: Teaching Company.

Gayton, A. 1948. Yokuts and Western Mono Ethnography. Berkeley, CA: University of California Press.

Gimbel, Steven. 2015. Redefining Reality: The Intellectual Implications of Modern Science. Chantilly, VA: Teaching Company.

Gordon, Alice. 2000. "Two Tales of a Zapotec Healer." Shaman's Drum 54 (Winter):12-22.

Grauds, Constance. 2001. "The Spirit Doctors of Ayahuasca." Shaman's Drum 60 (Fall):23-31.

Grimaldi, Susan. 2019. "Bringing Balance to the Moon." Sacred Hoop 102a:68l-77.

Grof, Stanislav. 2006. "Journeys into Shamanic Realities." Shaman's Drum 73:48-55.

Guggenheim, B., & J. Guggenheim. 1995. Hello from Heaven. New York, NY: Bantam.

Gunshore, Lisa. 2019. "Liberate Your Lineage." Sacred Hoop 104:47-49.

Gurr, Ted Robert. 1972. Polimetrics. Englewood Cliffs, NJ: Prentice-Hall.

Haebertin, Herman. 2019. "Trail to the Ghostlands: An Historic Account of an Early C20th Salish Sbeleda'q Soul Retrieval Ceremony." Sacred Hoop 101a:32-37.

Hallett, Elizabeth. 1995. Soul Trek: Meeting Our Children on the Way to Birth. N.p.: Light Hearts.

Handelman, Don. 1967. "The Development of a Washo Shaman." Ethnology 6,4 (October):444-464.

Harl, Kenneth. 2011. The Fall of the Pagans and the Origins of Medieval Christianity. Chantilly, VA: Teaching Company.

Harle, Christiana. 2019. "Pregnant with the Drum." Sacred Hoop 105:20-27.

Harner, Michael. 2006. "Tribal Wisdom and the Shamans." Shaman's Drum 71:16-24.

_____. 2008-2011. Three-Year Program in Advanced Shamanic Initiations, Foundation for Shamanic Studies at the Institute of Noetic Sciences, Petaluma, CA.

_____. 2010a. "A Core Shamanic Theory of Dreams." Shamanism Annual 23 (December):2-4.

_____. 2010b. "Shamanic Dreamwork." Workshop, Foundation for Shamanic Studies, San Francisco, CA, August.

Harris, Dean. 1919. Essays in Occultism, Spiritism, and Demonology. London, U.K.: B. Herder.

Haslund, Henning. 2019. "In the Darkness of the Tent." Sacred Hoop 102a:82-87.

Heaven, Ross. 2003. Vodou Shamanism. Rochester, VT: Destiny.

_____. 2018, "The Medsen Fey: The Leaf Doctors of Haiti." Sacred Hoop 100:80-85.

Hinze, Sarah. 1997. Coming from the Light: Spiritual Accounts of Life before Life. New York, NY: Gallery.

Hitchcock, John. 1967. "A Nepalese Shamanism and the Classic Inner Asian Tradition." History of Religions 7, 2 (November):149-158.

Holland, John. 2018. Bridging Two Realms: Learn to Communicate with Your Loved Ones on the Other Side. New York, NY: Hay House.

Host, Annette. 2018. "The Staff and the Song," Sacred Hoop 99:18-22.

Hurston, Zora. 1931. "Hoodoo in America." Journal of American Folklore 44, 174 (October-November):317-417.

Ingerman, Sandra. 2018. The Book of Ceremony: Shamanic Wisdom for Invoking the Sacred in Everyday Life. Boulder, CO: Sounds True.

Irwin, Louis Two Ravens. 1997. "Building Bridges beneath the Sacred Tree." Shaman's Drum 44 (March-May):21-26.

Isaacson, Rupert. 2009a. Horse Boy. New York, NY: Little, Brown.

_____. 2009b. "Riding with Horse Boy." Sacred Hoop 64:6-12.

Jonas, E., J. Schimel, S. Greenberg, & T. Pyszczynski. 2002. "The Scrooge Effect: Evidence That Mortality Salience Increases Prosocial Attitudes and Behavior." Personality and Social Psychology Bulletin 28:342-353.

Joy, Francis. 2009. "Repatriating Sami Shaman Drums." Shaman's Drum 80:8-9.

Kaldera, Raven, & Galina Krasskova. 2012. Neolithic Shamanism: Spirit Work in the Norse Tradition. Rochester, VT: Destiny.

Kane, Herb Kawainue. 2014. "The Aumakua–Hawaiian Ancestral Spirits." https://dinr.hawaii.gov/sharks/files/2014/07/apaperbyHerbKane.pdf Accessed 20 June 2019.

Katz, Richard. 1981. "Education as Transformation: Becoming a Healer among the! Kung and the Fijians." Harvard Education Review 51, 1 (February):57-78.

_____. 1999. The Straight Path of the Spirit: Ancestral Wisdom and Healing Traditions in Fiji. New York, NY: Park Street.

_____, M. Biesele, & V. St. Denis. 1997-1998. "Spiritual Healing among the Kalahari Ju|'hoansi." Shaman's Drum 47 (Winter):40-53.

Keeney, Bradford. 2003a. Ropes to God. Philadelphia, PA: Ringing Rocks.

_____. 2003b. "Singing and Praying with Guarani Shamans of the Rainforest." Shaman's Drum 64:16-21.

_____. 2005. "A Bushman Initiation." Shaman's Drum 68:44-52.

Kawabori, Kimi. 2019. "Ancestral Healing from an Adoptee's Perspective." Ancestral Healing Summit, Shift Network, www.theshiftnetwork.com Accessed 21 April.

Kendall, Laurel. 1988. "Healing Thyself: A Korean Shaman's Afflictions." Social Science and Medicine 27, 5:445-450.

Kim, Seong Nae. 1989. "Lamentations of the Dead: The Historical Imagery of Violence on Cheju Island, South Korea." Journal of Ritual Studies 3, 2 (Summer):254-285.

Kipp, Woody. 1996. "Learning to Trust the Spirits." Shaman's Drum 43 (Fall):21-25.

Koloko, Patience. 2002. "Zulu Healing." Workshop, International Herbal Symposium, Wheaton College, Norton, MA, July.

Kowalewski, David. 2000. Deep Power: The Political Ecology of Wilderness and Civilization. Huntington, NY: Nova Science.

_____. 2002a. Helping Students Go Feral: A University Course on Wild Edible and Medicinal Plants. Educational Research Quarterly 26, 2 (December):29-38.

_____. 2002b. "Teaching Deep Ecology: A Student Assessment." Journal of Environmental Education 33, 4 (Summer):20-27.

_____. 2007. "Plant-Spirit Medicine: Mystical Phytopharmaceuticals in an Old (and New) Key." Canadian Journal of Herbalism 27, 3 (Summer):3-18.

_____. 2008. "Eco-Mentoring: Using Nature as a Guide to Destiny." Australian Journal of Outdoor Education 12, 1:39-43.

_____. 2009. "Anatomy of a Wolf Den Site: A Field Report." Electronic Green Journal: A UCLA Publication 28

(Spring). http://repositories.cdlib.org/uclalib/egj/vol1/iss28/art1/

_____. 2012. "Real or Imaginex? Truth and Fiction in Shamanic Journeys." Journal of Shamanic Practice 5,2 (Fall):24-27.

_____. 2014. "The Call To Be a Shaman." Sacred Hoop 84:38-41.

_____. 2015, Death Walkers: Shamanic Psychopomps, Earthbound Ghosts, and Helping Spirits in the Afterlife Realm. Bloomington, IN: iUniverse.

_____. 2016. Destiny Retrieval: Shamanic Mentoring in the Age of Whatever. Bloomington, IN: iUniverse.

_____. 2019a. "The Shamanic Renaissance: What's Going On?" Journal of Humanistic Psychology 59, 2:170-184.

_____. 2019b. "Why Ancestors Matter." Ancestral Healing Summit, Shift Network, www.theshiftnetwork.com Accessed 21 April.

_____, C. Doucette, & P. Ransom. 2007. "Nature *and* Nurture." Children, Youth, Environments 17, 4:227-236.

Krippner, Stanley. 2008. "The Psychology of Shamanic Healing." Shaman's Drum 78:17-23.

_____, F. Bogzaran, & A. Percia de Carvalho. 2002. "Called to Be Dreamers." Shaman's Drum 61 (Spring):19-27.

LaFleur, Robert. 2015. Great Mythologies of the World. Chantilly, VA: Teaching Company.

Lecouteux, Claude. 2009. Return of the Dead: Ghosts, Ancestors, and the Transparent Veil of the Pagan Mind. Rochester, VT: Inner Traditions.

Lee, Patrick Jasper. 1999. "The Shamanic Ways of a Gypsy Chovihano." Shaman's Drum 51 (Spring) 30-39.

Lemoine, Jacques. 1996. "The Constitution of a Hmong Shaman's Powers of Healing and Folk Culture." Shaman 4, 1-2:143-165.

Linn, D., S. Linn, & M. Linn. 2016. The Gifts of Near-Death Experiences. Charlottesville, VA: Hampton Roads.

Little Eagle, Lionel. 2000. "Honoring Wakan Chanupa." Shaman's Drum 57 (Fall-Winter):47-59.

Lockley, John. 2017. Leopard Warrior: A Journey into the African Teachings of Ancestors, Instinct, and Dreams. Boulder, CO: Sounds True.

_____. 2019. "Way of the Leopard." Sacred Hoop 104:16-23.

Long, Jeffrey. 2010. Evidence of the Afterlife. New York, NY: HarperCollins.

_____, & Paul Perry. 2016. God and the Afterlife: The Groundbreaking New Evidence for God and the Near-Death Experience. New York, NY: HarperOne.

Lopez, S., J. Pedrotti, & C. Snyder. 2018. Positive-Psychology: The Scientific and Practical Explorations of Human Strengths. Thousand Oaks, CA: Sage.

Lorimer, D. 1929. "The Supernatural in the Popular Belief of the Gilgit Region." Journal of the Royal Asiatic Society:507-536.

Louis, Roberta. 1999. "Shamanic Healing Practices of the Ulchi." Shaman's Drum 53 (Fall):50-60.

_____. 2008. "Therapeutic Treatments Using Ibogaine: An Interview with Rocky Caravelli." Shaman's Drum 77:47-54.

Lundahl, Craig, & Harold Widdison. 1995. Eternal Journey: How Near-Death Experiences Illuminate Our Earthly Lives. New York, NY: Warner.

Luks, A. 1991. The Healing Power of Doing Good. New York, NY: Ballantine.

Luna, Luis. 2006. "The Role of Icaros, or Magical Chants, among Peru's Mestizo Shamans." Shaman's Drum 73:40-47.

Mabit, Jacques. 2006. "The Evolution of an Experimental Drug Treatment Program Using Ayahuasca." Shaman's Drum 73:22-31.

MacEowan, Frank. 1998. "Rekindling the Gaelic Hearthways of Oran Mor." Shaman's Drum 49 (Summer):33-39.

_____. 2001a. "MacEowen's Reply." Shaman's Drum 59 (Summer):8-10.

_____. 2001b. "Reclaiming Our Ancestral Bones: Revitalizing Shamanic Practices in the New Millennium." Shaman's Drum 58 (Spring):15-19.

MacLeod, Sharon. 2019. "From the Realm beneath the Waters." Sacred Hoop 102c:84-89.

Makransky, Bob. 2019. "Blessing the Flames: Quiche Mayan Fire Ceremonies." Sacred Hoop 102b:95-99.

Martin, Joel, & Patricia Romanowski. 1997. Love beyond Life: The Healing Power of After-Death Communication. New York, NY: Harper.

Martin, Stephan. 2008. "Indigenous Wisdom, Modern Science, and the Craft of Everyday Life." Shaman's Drum 78:5-7.

Martinez, Susan. 2019. Field Guide to the Spirit World. Rochester, VT: Bear.

Matthews, Caitlin. 2012. Celtic Visions. London, U.K.: Watkins.

_____. 2018. "Land and the Ancestors." Sacred Hoop 99:31-40.

Mathews, Patrick. 2019. Only a Thought Away: Keeping in Touch with Your Loved Ones in Spirit. Woodbury, MN: Llewellyn.

Maurey, Eugene. 1988. Exorcism. Westchester, PA: Whitford.

Mayatitinanda, Swamini. 2005. "Honoring Ancestors." Hinduism Today (July-September). www.hinduismtoday. com/modules/smartsection/item.php?itemid=1428 Accessed 21 September 2019

Menges, K. 1983. "Korean Shamanism." Central Asiatic Journal 27, 3-4:249-278.

Metzner, Ralph. 1999. "Ritual Approaches to Working with Sacred Medicine Plants: An Interview with Timothy White." Shaman's Drum 51 (Spring):19-29.

_____. 2008. "A Case of Ayahuasca Sorcery and Healing." Shaman's Drum 77:42-46.

Miller, Elmer. 1975. "Shamans, Power Symbols, and Change in Argentine Toba Culture." American Ethnologist 2, 3 (August):477-496.

Miro-Quesada, Oscar. 2019. "Shamanic Soul Medicine: Transforming the Past and Healing the Present." Ancestral Healing Summit, Shift Network, www.theshiftnetwork, com Accessed 21 April.

Miyake, Hitoshi. 1989. "Religious Rituals in Shugendo." Japanese Journal of Religious Studies 16, 2-3:101-116.

_____. 2001. Shugendo: Essays on the Structure of Japanese Folk Religion. Ann Arbor, MI: Center for Japanese Studies, University of Michigan.

Moses, Johnny. 1998. "Northwest Coast Medicine Teachings: An Interview with Timothy White." Shaman's Drum 50 (Winter) 40-46.

Moss, Robert. 1994. "An Active Dreaming Approach to Death, Dying, and Healing Dreams." Shaman's Drum 34 (Spring):17-23.

_____. 1998. "Blackrobes and Dreamers." Shaman's Drum 50 (Winter): 53-59.

_____. 2003. "The Healing Power of Ancient Iroquoian Dreamways." Shaman's Drum 64:54-65.

_____. 2006. "Dream Visitations with the Dead." Shaman's Drum 72:24-31.

Mottin, Jean. 1984. "A Hmong Shaman's Séance." Asian Folklore Studies 43:99-108.

Muesse, Mark. 2003. Great World Religions. Chantilly, VA: Teaching Company.

Musi, Carla. 1997. Shamanism from East to West. Budapest, Hungary: Academiai Kiado.

Nightingale, Christine. 2016. "Spirit Child." Sacred Hoop 91:35.

Noll, Richard, & Kun Shi. 2004. "Chuonnasuan (Meng Jin Fu): The Last Shaman of the Oroqen in Northeast China." Journal of Korean Religions 6:135-162.

Odigan, Sarangerel. 2018. "Children of the Wolf." Sacred Hoop 99:6-17.

Ohashi, H., S. Sakumichi, & K. Horike. 1984. "Social-Psychological Study of Okinawan Shamanism." Tohoku psychologica folia 43, 1-4:66-79.

Omega Institute. 2002, 2003. "Gathering of the Shamans." Workshops, Rhinebeck, NY, September.

Oschman, J. 2003. "Energy Medicine and the Revolution in Health Care." Address to the Green Nations Gathering, Rock Hill, NY, September.

_____. 2015. Energy Medicine: The Scientific Basis. Rushden, U.K.: Churchill Livingstone.

Paicheler, Agnes. 2008. "Holy Wood of the Ancestors: The Story of Iboga and Bwiti." Shaman's Drum 76:33-41.

Pallant, Cheryl. 2009. "The Shamanic Heritage of a Korean Mudang." Shaman's Drum 81:22-31.

Panthera, Leo. 2009. "When the Student Is Ready." Shaman's Drum 80:12-21.

Paper, Jordan. 1996. "Mediums and Modernity: The Institutionalization of Ecstatic Religious Functionaries in Taiwan." Journal of Chinese Religions 24, 1:105-129.

Park, Willard. 1934. "Paviotso Shamanism." American Anthropologist 36:98-113.

Parker, Z.A. 2010. "A Dress Made of Stars: A Description of a Ghost Dance." Sacred Hoop 67:27-29.

Paxson, Diana. 2015. Possession, Depossession, and Divine Relationships. San Francisco, CA: Weiser.

Pearson, Patricia. 2014. Opening Heaven's Door. New York, NY: Atria.

Perkins, John. 2001. "Dream Changing with Shuar Sacred Plants." Shaman's Drum 59 (Summer):18-27.

Peters, Larry. 1981, "An Experiential Study of Nepalese Shamanism." Journal of Transpersonal Psychology 13, 1:1-26.

_____. 1990. "Mystical Experience in Tamang Shamanism." ReVision 13, 2 (Fall):71-96.

_____. 1999. "The Day the Deities Return: The Janai Purnima Pilgrimage of Tamang Shamans." Shaman's Drum 52 (Summer): 40-49.

Pfeiffer, Bill. 2003. "Making Rainbows in Tuva." Shaman's Drum 64:30-39.

Pieper, 2007. "The Mayan Folk Saint Maximon/San Simon." Shaman's Drum 75:32-47.

Pollock, Donald. 2008. "Death and the Afterdeath among the Kulina." Latin American Anthropology Review 5, 2 (June):61-64,

Pratt, Christina. 2007. Encyclopedia of Shamanism, Vol. 1. New York, NY: Rosen.

_____. 2018. "The Power, Wisdom, and Protection of the Ancestors." Shamanism Summit, Sounds True, www.soundstrue.com Accessed 20 February.

_____. 2019a. "Ancestral Healing: We Can No Longer Afford to Wait to Be Ready." Ancestral Healing Summit, Shift Network, www.theshiftnetwork.com Accessed 21 April.

_____. 2019b. "Healing the Ancestral Lines." Workshop, Last Mask Center http://www.lastmaskcenter.org/workshops-classes/healing-ancestral-lines.htm Accessed 27 June.

_____. 2019c. "Healing with Your Ancestors: Elemental Rituals and Shamanic Practices to Transform Ancestral Suffering into Sacred Medicine." Online Seminar, Shift Network, https://theshift network.com Accessed 21 September.

Price, Neil. 2004. "The Archaeology of Seidr: Circumpolar Traditions in Viking Pre-Christian Religion." Brathair 4, 2:109-126.

Proud, L. 2015. Strange Electromagentic Dimensions: The Science of the Unexplainable. Pompton Plains, NJ: New Page.

Rasbold, Katrina. 2019. Crossroads of Conjure: The Roots and Practices of Granny Magic, Hoodoo, Brujeria, and Curanderismo. Woodbury, MN: Llewellyn.

Raven Wing, Josie. 1997-1998. "Return to Spirit: An Interview with Roberta Louis." Shaman's Drum 47 (Winter):54-64.

_____. 2001. "Joao de Deus, the Miracle Man of Brazil." Shaman's Drum 58 (Spring):34-45.

Reese, Whitney, & Stuart Boag. 2008. "Ongon: A Home for a Spirit." Sacred Hoop 61:28-30.

Riboli, Diana. 1994. "Shamanic Rites of the Terai Chepangs." East and West 44, 1-2 (December):327-352.

_____. 2002. "Trances of Initiation, Incorporation, and Movement: Three Different Typologies of the Shamanic Trance." Shaman 10, 1-2 (Spring-Autumn):161-180.

Riccio, Thomas. 1996, "Today We Sing! Healing Rituals of the !Xuu and Khwe Bushmen." Shaman's Drum 42 (Summer):42-54.

Ring, Kenneth. 2006. Lessons from the Light: What We Can Learn from the Near-Death Experience. Needham, MA: Moment Point.

Robinson, Dana. 1998. "Death, Dying, and Beyond." Workshop, Foundation for Shamanic Studies, Altoona, PA, 12-13 September.

Roland, Paul. 2012. Ghosts. London, U.K.: Arcturus.

Rowan, L., J. Lindsay, J. Moore, & A. Shoemaker. 1999. "Community Health Workers Examining the Helper Therapy Principle." Public Health Nursing 16, 2:87-95.

Rubin, Amalia. 2019a. "An Outsider on the Inside." Sacred Hoop 102a:88-93.

_____. 2019b. "Relinquishing to the Divine." Sacred Hoop 102a:42-46.

Ryan, Robert. 1999. The Strong Eye of Shamanism. Rochester, VT: Inner Traditions.

Sacred Hoop. 2007. "The Lore of Iron." 58:22-23.

_____. 2013. "Walking in the Dreamtime." 81:26-27.

_____. 2019a. "Bundles of Power: A Brief Introduction to Q'ero Style Mesas." 102b:92-94.

_____. 2019b. "Spirits of the Southern Seas." 102:36-41.

Sartori, Penny. 2014. The Wisdom of Near-Death Experiences. London, UK: Watkins.

Schiavi, Brooke. 2018. "Living in a Glass House: An Interview with Oglala Medicine Man David Swallow." Sacred Hoop 99:58-63.

Schinzinger, Annelise. 2008. "Enlightened by Hoasca." Shaman's Drum 78:24-31.

Scott, Michel, & Rupert Isaacson. 2009. Horse Boy. New York, NY: Zeitgeist Films.

Shaman's Drum. 2000. "Master of the Drum: A Buryat Shaman's Chant." Winter:31-39.

Sheat, W. W. 1902. "Wild Tribes of the Malay Peninsula." Journal of the Anthropological Institute of Great Britain and Ireland 32 (January-June):124-141.

Sheldrake, Rupert. 2018. "Morphic Resonance, Psychedelic Experience, and Collective Memory." Pp. 205-224 in David Luke & Rory Spowers (eds.), DMT Dialogues: Encounters with the Spirit Molecule. Rochester, VT: Park Street.

Sidky, M. 1994. "Shamans and Mountain Spirits in Hunza." Asian Studies Journal 53:67-96.

Silvana, Laura. 2009. Plant Spirit Journey. Woodbury, MN: Llewellyn.

Simonsen, Torstein. 2019. "The Mountain and the Song." Sacred Hoop 105:40-45.

Sims, Lisa. 2019. "Q'ero 101." Sacred Hoop 102b:72-79.

Smith, Gordon. 2018. Through My Eyes: A Medium Reveals the Reassuring Truth about the Afterlife. New York, NY: Hay House.

Smith, Willie, & Esme Ryan. 1999. Spirit of the First People: Native American Music Traditions of Washington State. Seattle, WA: University of Washington Press.

Sodnom, Munkhbat. 2019. "Sitting beneath the Amulet Tree." Sacred Hoop 102a:94-100.

Some, Malidome. 1997. "The Gift of Medicine." Workshop, Omega Institute, Rhinebeck, NY, May. With Robert Bly.

Staley, John. 1982. Words for My Brother. Karachi, Pakistan: Oxford University Press.

Stavis, Rachel. 2018. Sister of Darkness: The Chronicles of a Modern Exorcist. New York, NY: Day Street.

Stern, David. 2012. "Masters of Ecstasy." National Geographic (December):110-131.

Stevens, Karen. 2007. Haunted Montana: A Ghost Hunter's Guide. Helena, MT: Riverbend.

_____. 2010. More Haunted Montana: Haunted Places You Can Visit. Helena, MT: Riverbend.

Stone, Daniel. 2019. "Walking until the End of the World: A Sacred Landscape under Threat in Mexico." Sacred Hoop 102b:100-103.

Sutherland, Cherie. 1989. "Psychic Phenomena Following Near-Death Experiences." Journal of Near-Death Studies 8, 2 (Winter):93-102.

Talmadge, Candace, & Jana Simons. 2015. The Afterlife Healing Circle: How Anyone Can Contact the Other Side. Pompton Plains, NJ: Career.

Tedlock, Barbara. 2005. The Woman in the Shaman's Body. New York, NY: Bantam-Dell.

———. 2006. "Grandmother's Wisdom." Shaman's Drum 72:16-23.

Tein, Tassan. 1994. "Shamans of the Siberian Eskimos." Arctic Anthropology 31, 1:117-125.

Thomas, Lesley. 2018. "Visions of the End of Days: Eskimo Shamanism in Northwest Alaska." Sacred Hoop 101a:20-25.

Thornton, John. 1988. "On the Trail of Voodoo: African Christianity in Africa and the Americas." The Americas 44, 3 (January):261-278.

Tkacz, Virlana. 2002. Shamans and the Dedication Ritual of a Buryat Shaman in Siberia. New York, NY: Park Street.

———. 2016. Siberian Shamanism: The Shanar Ritual of the Buryats. Rochester, VT: Inner Traditions.

Todd, Donna. 2010. "Between Heaven and Earth: Mongolian Shamans Today." Shaman's Drum 82:22-39.

Townsley, Graham. 1993. "Song Paths: The Ways and Means of Yaminahua Shamanic Knowledge." L'Homme 33, 126-128:449-468.

Turner, Kevin. 2019. "Touching the Primordial Roots: Meetings with Mongolian Darkhad Shamans." Sacred Hoop 102a: 17-25.

Van der Linden, S. 2011. "The Helper's High: Why It Feels So Good to Give." Ode Magazine 8, 6:26-27.

van Deusen, Kira. 1997-1998. "Shamanism and Music in Tuva and Khakassia." Shaman's Drum 47 (Winter):22-29.

_____. 2005. "The Shamanic Use of Sound in Tuva." Shaman's Drum 68:17-23.

Vandiver, Elizabeth. 2014. "The Histories." Track 6 in Audio CD, Thirty-Six Books That Changed the World. Chantilly, VA: Teaching Company.

van Praagh, James. 2009. Unfinished Business. New York, NY: HarperOne.

van Ysslestyne, Jan. 2019a. "Generosity and Hospitality: Healing and Self-Healing among the Ulchi Shamans of the Amur River Region." Sacred Hoop 102a:118-121.

_____. 2019b. "People of the Tiger." Sacred Hoop 103:12-18.

Vaudoise, Vallorie. 2019. Honoring Your Ancestors: A Guide to Ancestral Veneration. Woodbury, MN: Llewellyn.

Villoldo, A. 1996. "Inca Shamanism: Soul Retrieval Intensive." Workshop, Omega Institute, Rhinebeck, NY, May.

Voth, Grant. 2015. Great Mythologies of the World. Chantilly, VA: Teaching Company.

Wahbeh, Helane. 2019. "IONS Channeling Research Program." Reuniting Science and Spirituality Summit, https://noetic.org/research/ions-channeling-research-program/ Accessed 13 August.

Wands, Jeffrey. 2006. Another Door Opens: A Psychic Explains How Those in the World of Spirit Continue to Impact Our Lives. New York, NY: Atria.

White, Timothy. 2005. "Revisioning Siberian Shamanisms." Shaman's Drum 69:42-54.

_____. 2006. "Psychedelic Poisons Aren't the Same as Shamanic Sacraments." Shaman's Drum 72:49-54.

Wilcox, Joan. 2004. Masters of the Living Energy: The Mystical World of the Q'ero of Peru. Rochester, VT: Inner Traditions.

Williams, James. 1999. "Dona Tonia: A Mexican-Yaqui Curandera," Shaman's Drum 53 (Fall):40-50.

_____. 2007. "Offerings for Pachamama: My Initiation into Q'ero Shamanism." Shaman's Drum 74:31-42.

Winders, R. 1994. "The Awakener and the Dancer: The Jagar of the Kumaon Himalayas." Shaman's Drum 36 (Fall):32-39.

Winkelman, Michael, & Philip Peek. 2004. Divination and Healing. Tucson, AZ: University of Arizona Press.

Winter, Ellen, & Mohan Rai. 2000. "The Shaman of Dorokha Conquers the Bokshies." Shaman's Drum 54 (Winter):23-29.

Wolynn, Mark. 2017. It Didn't Start with You: How Inherited Family Trauma Shapes Who We Are. New York, NY: Penguin.

_____. 2019. "It Didn't Start with You: How to Break the Cycle of Inherited Family Trauma." Reuniting Science and Spirituality Summit https://noetic.org/research Accessed 13 August.

Wood, Nicholas Breeze. 2006. "Tales of the Djinn: The Spirits & Beings of Islam." Sacred Hoop 51:19-21.

_____. 2014. "Spirit of the Blacksmith." Sacred Hoop 81:44-47.

_____. 2019a. "Angakok: The Shamans of Greenland." Sacred Hoop 101a:26-31.

_____. 2019b. "Shamans at the Center of the World." Sacred Hoop 102a:102-109.

_____. 2019c. "The Siberian Shaman's 'Dudig' Apron." Sacred Hoop 102a:101.

Wright, James. 1997. "A Cauldron-Born Quest." Shaman's Drum 46 (Fall):50-59.

Wright, Sylvia. 1999. "Paranormal Contact with the Dying." Journal of the Society for Psychical Research 63, 857 (October):258-267.

_____. 2006. "Candles, Incense, and Contact with the Dead," Journal of Spirituality and Paranormal Studies 16:197-201.

About the Author

Dr David Kowalewski has been researching, teaching, and practicing shamanism for 25 years. Twice a Fulbright scholar, twice a National Foreign Language fellow, and twice a National Endowment for the Humanities grantee, he has also received stipends from NASA, Alfred P. Sloan Foundation, several universities, and other institutions. His teachers have included shamans of many continents, and his reports have appeared in the *Journal of Contemporary Shamanism, Journal of Shamanic Practice, Journal of Transpersonal Psychology, Journal of Humanistic Psychology, Sacred Hoop, Journal for the Scientific Study of Religion, Review of Religious Research, Sociology of Religion,* and elsewhere. His research on developing societies has been published in *Ethnic Groups, Ethnic and Racial Studies, Asian Survey, Peasant Studies,* and other journals, and his work has been translated into several languages. He has been interviewed by *Chronicle of Higher Education, National Geographic,* Associated Press, Canadian Broadcasting Corporation, National Public Radio, and other platforms. He is a graduate of the Foundation for Shamanic Studies' Three-Year Program in Advanced Shamanic Initiation at the Institute of Noetic Sciences. He has been featured on the *Shift Network*'s global online summit, "Healing the Ancestors"; the *Why Shamanism Now*'s podcast, "Psychopomp Work"; and several other sites.

ALSO BY DAVID KOWALEWSKI:

Destiny Retrieval: Shamanic Mentoring in the Age of Whatever (iUniverse, 2016)

Praise for *Destiny Retrieval*

Modern society, Kowalewski asserts . . . pushes individuals . . . away from a deep engagement with compassion, purpose, and service. His book begins by delving into a discussion of life's purpose and the trajectory of the human journey. Shamans . . . are the world's "oldest soul doctors," who align clients with the purposes and meanings of their lives. . . . The author explains at length in an orderly set of chapters how shamanism and mentorship have lost meaning and prevalence . . . due to . . . an oversaturation of consumerism, and . . . an "inadequate initiation of the young into the tribe." What have replaced them . . . are "ego mentors"—psychotherapists, self-help therapists, and life coaches—who provide "mood boosts" that fail to compare to the deep spiritual guidance of shamans. . . . Shamans . . . have transcendent relationships with the gods . . . to guide clients away from . . . false identities, the negative power of words, and attachments to the past. The author . . . offers what many books in the mystical genre lack: a clear, concise, well-organized depiction of the challenges of spirituality in contemporary life ("Modernism, instead of treating life as a hero's quest for spiritual significance, has encouraged a professional's career for economic advancement. We are taught promotion of self instead of service to others"). Any reader who wants . . . a deeper understanding of the self . . . should enjoy this thought-provoking work's lucid focus. Kowalewski successfully presents succinct and simple explanations of the mystical possibilities of a deeper spiritual journey. A useful and intellectually stimulating manual aimed at readers yearning to find their destinies.

–KIRKUS REVIEWS

Printed in the United States
By Bookmasters